Archway Publishing books may be ordered through booksellers or by contacting:

Archway Publishing
1663 Liberty Drive
Bloomington, IN 47403
www.archwaypublishing.com
844-669-3957

ISBN: 978-1-6657-4638-0 (sc)
ISBN: 978-1-6657-4639-7 (e)

Library of Congress Control Number: 2023912096

Print information available on the last page.

Archway Publishing rev. date: 07/31/2023

I STAND BEFORE YOU a Florida HVAC Contractor WHO:

    a. refuses to allow the suffering of his American people to proceed uncontested

    b. loves teaching others what the universe has blessed him with

    c. is looking to pay his immense debt to the universe effective immediately

I HAVE DEDICATED MY ENTIRE LIFE passionately teaching my Florida Homeowners and Renters exactly HOW TO:

    a. identify ways they unknowingly consume obscene amounts of energy

    b. employ simple protocols & procedures to rapidly reduce energy consumption

    c. eradicate monthly excessively high power bills with Extreme Prejudice

THROUGH THE PUBLICATION AND PROMOTION of this Definitive Guide I SHARE THE:

    a. helix of my DNA with every American suffering the indigent despair of dire straits

    b. the ancient protection & wisdom the universe has repeatedly bestowed upon me

BY Page Four (4) YOU WILL EASILY LEARN:

    a. Procedures & Protocols to Reduce Power Bills By 12% to 16%.

BY Page Nine (9) YOU WILL UNDERSTAND AND RETAIN:

    a. First-Hand Knowledge to Reduce Power Bills By 19% to 24%.

BY Page Twelve (12) YOU WILL FOREVER COMPREHEND:

> *a. Techniques & Strategies to Reduce Power Bills 35% to 42%.*

BY Page(15) YOU WILL ABSOLUTELY MASTER:

> *a. Contingencies & Countermeasures to Reduce Power Bills By 46% to 56%.*

By The Last Page YOU WILL FIND YOURSELF:

> *a. prepared to share what you have learned with everyone you love.*
> *b. prepared to never waste energy, money, life on routine high power bills*

My name is: John Rubio. I am the son of Carlos Rubio & Marisol Chavez. I am the father of Christian Rubio. I was created in compassion & kindness to publish a book THAT WILL:

> *a. free millions of bleeding Americans' from the inhumane covert enslavement of high-power bills*
> *b. effortlessly teach every American to eradicate their high power bills with extreme prejudice & absolute accuracy*

Thank you for having me in your home. I welcome every single one of you to my Life's work....

*ARE YOU READY ....Well Then, Step Into My Office Please... You Are Now Reading: **The Simple Art of Reducing Energy Consumption -The Definitive Guide-***

It is this; State of Florida Licensed Air Conditioning Contractor's Opinion that:

"...NO ONE IN OUR NATION IS SPARED RAPIDLY RISING 2023 ENERGY COST... IT'S ALMOST AS IF ROUTINE HIGH-POWER BILLS ARE DEVOURING AMERICANS ALIVE, SOMETHING MUST BE DONE, NOW..."

-John Rubio--June 1ˢᵗ, 2023, Tampa Bay, Florida -

1. *This Comprehensive Definitive Guide Will Include:*
    a. *Objective Testing, Theory & Amp Draw Explanation*
    b. *4-Steps to Reduce Energy Consumption*
    c. *Trade Knowledge Applications to Reduce Energy Consumption in Perpetuity*
    d. *Emergency Energy Consumption Reduction Procedures & Protocols*

2. *4-Step Theory to Dominate Power Bills is Hereinafter Defined, Set Forth & Established by John Rubio, CAC1818897 pro-se litigant on the 1ˢᵗ Day of June 2023*

3. *Trade Knowledge Applications to Reduce Energy Consumption in Perpetuity Hereinafter Defined, Set Forth & Established By John Rubio, CAC1818897 pro-se litigant on the 1ˢᵗ Day of June 2023*

4. *Emergency Energy Consumption Reduction Procedures Hereinafter Defined, Set Forth & Established by John Rubio, CAC1818897 pro-se litigant on the 1ˢᵗ Day of June, 2023*

*1(e) Mr. Rubio's Aforementioned Credentials not only bears a significant relationship to, but is inter-alia Inextricably Intertwined with the publication, **The Simple Art of Reducing Energy Consumption –The Definitive Guide-***

5. *.... TAKEAWAY I....THE KEYS TO UNLOCKING YOUR POWER-BILLS ARE WAITING FOR YOU INSIDE YOUR POWER METER....*

6. *Power meters in our homes used to have an "old school" type of meter that was equipped with a spinning disk....*

7. *This spinning disk was used by your power company to measure how much energy was consumed every month....*

8. *This spinning disk would spin faster when lots of energy was being consumed....*

9. *This spinning disk would spin slower when less energy was being consumed....*

10. *This spinning disk was measuring the amp draw of your home....*

11. *Amp draw is remarkably simple to understand....*

12. *Electrical appliances consuming voltage (plugged-in) & performing work (Fan spinning) produce amp draw.*

13. *.... SIMPLE EXAMPLES:*
    a. *light bulb on (performing work) will typically draw 1-amp*
    b. *ceiling fan spinning (performing work) will typically draw 3-amps*
    c. *blender on (performing work) will typically draw 4-amps*
    d. *hair dryer drying (performing work) will typically draw 12 amps*
    e. *toaster toasting (performing work) will typically draw 5-amps*

14. *.... TAKEAWAY II ANY ELECTRICAL APPLIANCE OR DEVICE PLUGGED INTO YOUR WALL (THAT IS ON) WILL PRODUCE AN AMP DRAW...*

15. *.... TAKEAWAY III WE MEASURE AMP DRAW WITH HAND-HELD ELECTRICAL MULTI-METERS EQUIPPED WITH AMP CLIPS*

16. *YOU NOW UNDERSTAND FIVE (5) CONCEPTS:*

    a. electrical appliances and devices consuming voltage (plugged in) and (performing work) produce an amp draw

    b. handheld electrical multi- meters equipped with amp clips are used in the field to measure amp draw

    c. Electrical meters in our homes measure the amp draw of our electrical devices and appliances.

    d. the higher the amp draw the faster the meter spins

    e. the lower the amp draw the slower the meter spins

17. *TAKEAWAY IV. AMP DRAW CAN BE SIMPLY DEFINED AS THE MEASUREMENT OF ENERGY CONSUMPTION.*

18. *TAKEAWAY V. HIGHER THE AMP DRAW OF ANY ELECTRICAL APPLIANCE THE FASTER METER WILL SPIN.... LOWER THE AMP DRAW OF ANY ELECTRICAL APPLIANCE THE SLOWER METER WILL SPIN.*

19. *I am about to say one (1) thing three (3) different ways. stay sharp:*

    a. electrical appliances that produce intense heat also produce the highest amp draw

    b. electrical appliances in your home that produce the highest amp draw also produce intense heat

    c. highest amp draws in your home are produced by the electrical appliances that also produce intense heat.

20. *WE MUST UNDERSTAND:*

a. *a high amp draw denotes a large consumption of energy that makes the **meter spin faster.***

b. *a low amp draw denotes a small consumption of energy that makes the **meter spin slower.***

c. *residential power meters in every U.S. **city measure amp draw.***

d. *higher amp draws force the meter to spin faster and faster and faster.*

e. *lower amp draws force the meter to spin slower and slower and slower.*

f. *amp draws are measured by handheld multi-meters equipped with amp clips.*

g. *electrical appliances that produce intense heat also produce the highest amp draw.*

21. ***Absolutely well done! You now understand crucial amp draw basics...we are now ready for step 1***

STEP ONE(1)

WHICH HOME APPLIANCE PRODUCES THE SINGLE LARGEST AMP DRAW? WHICH APPLIANCE HURTS US MOST? WHICH ELECTRICAL APPLIANCE IS STEADY ABUSING YOU EVERY SINGLE TIME YOUR FEED YOUR FAMILY....?

Lets Talk

TURKEY

"KNOW THY ENEMY" - Sun Tzu - The Art of War

Three (3) easy quick concepts...Ears up, Eyes open, Can't Lose, The professor is in, We start with:

a. UNIFORMITY ACROSS THE UNITED STATES
b. 120-VOLTS VS 240-VOLTS
c. RESIDENTIAL HEATING ELEMENTS

22. **What *is* NATIONWIDE UNIFORMITY IN CONSTRUCTION TRADES?**

23. *Uniformity is Easy.... Renters typically live in multi-family housing residential apartment communities. Homeowners typically live in single- family residential communities.*

24. *Multi-Family Residences typically DO have walls that are shared with neighbors*

25. *Single-Family Residences typically DO NOT have walls that are shared with neighbors.*

26. *Do Not Get Hung Up on the aspect of renting.... Families purchase condominiums, townhouses, and villas in multi-family housing communities every single day.... Tenants rent single-family stand-alone homes nationwide....*

27. *It Is Not About Renting.... It is about you seeing that through nationwide uniformity in the construction trades.... Everything inside of our homes/apartments is exactly the same....*

28. *This Means the Same residential electrical appliances in single-family/multi-family homes in my city are the same electrical appliances in single- family/multi-family homes nationwide....*

29. *Quick Example... This is a big nation; however, breaker-boxes in our homes are identical specifications such as wire gauge and safety ratings.*

30. *Electrical Wires in Walls of nationwide multi-family & single-family homes are Identical.*

31. *Handheld Electrical Multi-Meters equipped with amp clips read the same amp draws from the same electrical appliances regardless of city/state.*

32. *The Same Breakers Sold In Seattle stores are the same breakers sold in Florida*

33. *New Construction Building Codes are established & enforced in the name of nationwide uniformity… Always have been… Since black & white TV*

34. *County Code Inspectors Inspect new construction for nationwide uniformity*

35. *All This to Say…. The same unchecked electrical appliances causing you astronomical power bills are the exact same appliances I have repaired, serviced, & whispered to over an entire lifetime….*

36. *Through The Simple Art of Reducing Energy Consumption…. You Now Understand That:*

    a. *Residential Housing in the U.S. is divided between single-family housing and multi-family housing.*

    b. *Residential Housing Regardless of single-family/multi-family nationwide have identical electrical appliances*

    c. *Residential New Construction trade inspectors pass permits for work completed in nationwide uniformity*

    d. *Nationwide Uniformity Clearly Confirms the pragmatic protocols & procedures Contained in this Definitive Guide Apply to Every Single Residential Electrical Appliance…. in Every Single Residential Home… Nationwide… For the Extremely Foreseeable Future*

37. *120-VOLTS VS 240-VOLTS with special guest appearance of 208-Volts.... Super Easy Simple Stuff....*

38. *We Start Again with Nationwide Uniformity.... We know that because of nationwide construction trade uniformity everything is the same.... Thus, we start our voltage lesson in any U.S. city.*

39. *Every typical Residential Home has high voltage wires that enter the home through the power meter then to the breaker box.*

40. *Every U.S. home Has the Same typical breaker box that receives three (3) physical wires from local power companies.*

41. *Two (2) of the Three (3) Wires provide voltage, the third wire DOES NOT provide voltage.*

42. *Each Wire That Has Voltage provides 120 volts and is known as one (1) leg of power/voltage.*

43. *Most Electrical Appliances in our home require one (1) leg of voltage to perform work (TV is on)*

44. *Wall Receptacles provide 120-volts Or one (1) leg of power to electrical appliances/devices.*

45. *Heavy Duty Electrical Appliances that produce heat require 240 volts Or two (2) legs of power*

46. *240-Volts Is a Requirement for electrical appliances that Produce Intense Heat.... 208 volts is also two (2) legs of power with slightly less voltage in each leg. 208 is forbidden in single-family homes and is rarely found in much older multi-family housing such as high rise condominiums.*

47. *It is Crucial to Understand Every Major Electrical Appliance that produces heat in our homes requires 240 volts/two legs of power to perform work....*

48. *Through The Simple Art of Reducing Energy Consumption You Now Understand That:*

a. *ALL Residential Homes Nationwide receive two legs of power from power companies.*

b. *Our Electrical Appliances and Devices require one (1) or (2) legs of power to perform work.*

c. *Residential Heavy Duty electrical appliances that produce heat require both legs Or 240-volts of power to perform work.*

d. *Residential 240-Volt Appliances that Produce Heat also Produce the Highest Amp Draw as theyCommand/ Force/ Induce the Meter to Spin Faster*

e. *208 Volts Will Rarely Be Found in Multi-Family housing buildings and NEVER in single-family buildings.... All due to Nationwide Uniformity*

49. *Now We Close Our Step-1 intro lessons with HEATING ELEMENTS.... Know Thy Enemy...*

50. *We Have Learned That.... Electrical appliances that produce heat also produce the highest amp draw and force the power meter to spin fast & hard.*

51. *Heating Elements Are Used Daily by our homes electrical appliances to feed our families.*

52. *Heating Elements Are Everywhere.... When we push down on the toaster and see those glowing red coils, those are heating elements.... A standard light bulb contains a tiny heating element known as a tungsten filament.*

53. *Smaller Heating Elements produce less amp draw than large heating elements. Curling irons & hair dryers plug into receptacles & consume one (1) leg of voltage to perform work with heating elements.*

54. *U.S. Residential Heating Elements are rated to consume either 120 volts Or 240 volts.*

55. *Our Residential Heating Elements are the primary reason our power meters spin fast all day.*

56. *Our Electrical Appliances That Hurt Us with astronomical high monthly power bills Consume/ Eat/ Use two (2) legs of power /240 Volts TO COME TO LIFE...*

57. *Our Electrical Appliances That Hurt Us then use 240-Volt Heating Elements To STARVE US To DEATH....*

58. *A Wise Man Once Said,* **"Know Thy Enemy"***....*

59. *I Say.... "No Flippin Problem".... Not Even a Little Bit....*

60. *Through The Simple Art of Reducing Energy Consumption You Now Understand That:*

    a. *ALL Residential Homes Nationwide receive two legs of power from power companies*

    b. *Heating Elements are used to produce intense heat in our homes*

    c. *Heating Elements are rated 120 volts or 240 volts depending on how many legs of voltage are required to perform work*

    d. *120 volts equals 1 leg of power.*

    e. *240 volts equals 2 legs of power*

    f. *Heating Elements are big & small and are used in every U.S. kitchen to feed American families daily*

    g. *Electrical Appliances that produce the highest amp draw are typically rated for 240 volts as (2) legs of voltage/ 240V are required to cook*

    h. *Electrical power meters in our homes measure the amp draw produced by our electrical appliances & devices.*

    i. *Our Spinning Disk Spins Faster when 240-volt heating elements are consuming two (2) legs of voltage and performing work.*

j. *Heating Elements Are Used Daily by our homes electrical appliances to feed our families and so much more.*

61. *TAKEAWAY XV(15) ON A TYPICAL TURKEY DAY, UP TO FIVE (5) HEATING ELEMENTS IN THE FORM OF ONE (1) BAKE ELEMENT & FOUR (4) STOVE BURNERS.... GLOW CHERRY RED.... WITH YUMMY SIDES TO COMPLIMENT THE BIG TURKEY IN THE OVEN...*

62. *Americans' Consume Obscene Amounts of Energy on Turkey Day Because Electric Range Oven Nationwide will be:*

    a. *Consuming 240-volts to perform work by producing the intense heat needed to cook a raw turkey*

    b. *Producing a Typical 47 Amp Draw as up to five (5) multiple heating elements is consuming two (2) legs of high voltage to produce the intense heat needed to cook a raw Turkey and all the yummy sides....*

    c. *Forcing Power Meters to spin faster than usual as all four (4) electric heating elements in the form of stovetop burners are glowing cherry red whilst the electric heating element in the form of a large bake element is cooking the Turkey itself....*

    d. *Consuming More energy than usual as the electric range oven has four (4) individual heating elements glowing cherry red to compliment the large glowing red baking element inside the oven*

    e. *Performing the Work they were designed/ engineered/created and intended for...*

63. *Electric Range Ovens Consume Enormous Amounts of Energy As They Are:*

    a. *Designed to Effortlessly Produce the intense heat required to cook a turkey and sides daily.*

b. *Mass Produced with Six (6) separate heating elements required to cook a turkey and sides daily.*

c. *Obligated to Consume the 240-Volts of voltage required to cook a turkey & sides nonstop, back-to-back, every day*

d. *Extremely Outdated as advancement in technology over the last forty years now allows intense heat to be produced consuming, I leg of power/120-V instead of both legs of power/240-V*

e. *an Ancient Relic from a Pre-World War I era built when a loaf of bread cost eight (8) pennies.*

f. *an Extremely Powerful Electric range oven invented to cook full size turkeys not fish sticks*

g. *a Brute Machine Built to separate cavemen from civilized society in the late 1800s.*

h. *The Perfect Way to Cook Food Daily…. in 1934*

64. *ELECTRIC RANGE OVENS "HAVE" & WILL" HAVE ALWAYS" …. PRODUCED THE MOST HEAT IN EVERY TYPICAL U.S. HOME… AMP DRAW =47-AMPS*

65. *ANY ELECTRICAL APPLIANCE PRODUCING INTENSE HEAT <u>ALSO</u> PRODUCES EXTREMELY HIGH AMP DRAW ALL YEAR LONG….*

66. *HUMAN BEINGS WILL LOSE EVERY SINGLE TIME they use their full-size electric range oven to cook small food **such as:***

a. *frozen pizza, chicken pot pies, pizza rolls, **baked goods,** garlic toast, **hash browns,** oats, **noodles, rice, chili,** ox-tail **meat loaf,** pot roast, **mozzarella, jello, fish sticks, hot potatoes, pancakes,** oils, **omelets, potatoes, vegetables,** hot dogs, **gizzards, spareribs, shaved yak,** cheeseburgers, **tacos, nachos, lasagna,** stuffed bell peppers,**canned soup,** racks of ribs,*

London broil, pork chops ham-hocks, hot Coa-coa chimi-changas, mashed fully loaded potatoes, tilapia, fajitas, pot roast, french- fries, yams, mystery meat, tofu, quail, pheas-ant,.... bacon too... et cetera...

67. *YOUR FAMILY LOSES the INSTANT you PREHEAT YOUR ELECTRIC RANGE OVEN TO COOK ANYTHING EXCEPT A danged turkey!!!*

68. *Please Be Advised That Your Electric Range Oven* **STRAIGHT UP:**
    a. *Does Not Care about you or your entire family*
    b. *Demands 240-V of electricity to produce heat*
    c. *Was Invented to cook turkeys... not dino nuggets*
    d. *Forces You to Spend money on HIGH BILLS*

69. *Its Noteworthy to Mention Your Favorite Electric Range Oven* **ABSOLUTELY:**
    a. *Cannot Tell & DOES NOT CARE if you are cooking a twenty(20lbs) pound turkey or a hot pocket*
    b. *Produces The Same astronomical amp draw regardless of what's cooking every single day...*
    c. *KEEPS the meter spinning fast and hard three (3) times a day, seven (7) days out of week, so on and so forth.... till you move out.... to go meet your new stove...*
    d. *KEEPS YOU spending an extra four ($4) dollars in energy cost to heat up your go-to eighty-nine (89) cent frozen beef & bean burrito every single time*

70. *When you are Consistently Frequently ALWAYS cooking your Daily Meals with your electric range oven, then that means You Are Consistently Frequently* **ALWAYS:**

a. *Consuming Excessive Extremely Exorbitant Expensive Energy for Absolutely Nothing for Decades…*

b. *Producing a typical 47-Amp Draw as you cook slices of bologna, brownies…. Over the Last few Years…*

c. *Commanding your meter to spin fast over tater- tots, French fries…. Over This Past Year Solid….*

d. *Taxing yourself six ($6) when cooking a two ($2) pack of scalloped potatoes… Over The Past Months…*

e. *Paying Nearly five ($5) dollars in nightly energy cost cooking tons of discount cake mix Just Last Week*

f. *Starving over your lunch break Today for the third (3rd) time this week…& Half of Last Week too*

g. *Spending Next Month's grocery money on this month's excessive routine high-power bill*

h. *Bringing Home Less & Less Food Tomorrow*

i. *Tired Angry and Hungry as you plead for more over time at work to get the high bills covered*

71. *TAKEAWAY XIV(14) SMALL FOODS COOKED INSIDE ELECTRIC RANGE OVENS WASTE EIGHTY (80%) PERCENT OF THE ENERGY REQUIRED TO PRODUCE OVENS INTENSE HEAT*

72. *TAKEAWAY XII(12) HOMEOWNERS & RENTERS…. COOKING SMALL FOOD IN THEIR ELECTRIC RANGE OVEN WILL LOSE EVERY SINGLE TIME…*

73. *Cooking For Your Family every single day with a electric range oven means YOUR FAMILY:*

a. *LOST the Instant You Preheat Your Electric Range Oven….*

b. *IS LOSING with Each & Every Single Meal…*

c. *IS LOSING Three (3x) Times a Day*

    d. *IS LOSING Each & Every Day of the Week*

    e. *WILL LOSE Every Single Month All YEAR LONG*

74. *TAKEAWAY XIV (14) THE SIMPLE PERMANENT FIX IS TO PURCHASE THE SMALLEST POSSIBLE COUNTERTOP BAKING OVEN AND THE SMALLEST POSSIBLE COUNTERTOP COOKSURFACE EFFECTIVE IMMEDIATELY*

75. *TAKEAWAY XV (15)... COUNTER-TOP OVENS AND COOK SURFACES.... TYPICALLY REDUCE COOKING /BAKING ENERGY CONSUMPTION BY EIGHTY (80%) PERCENT....*

76. *Countertop Ovens and Cook Surfaces will reduce your energy consumption immediately as they are* **DESIGNED TO EFFICIENTLY:**

    a. *Consume only 120-volts of electricity to produce intense heat instead of the 240 volts*

    b. *produce a typical 8-amps to bake/cook instead of the typical 47-amps of your full size electric range oven*

    c. *command/force/induce the meter to spin five(5x) times slower when baking/cook reduce the original excessive 47- amps way down to an efficient 8-amps*

    d. *utilize advancements in technology that allows for intense heat to be produced without the antiquated requirement of both (2) legs of power/240*

77. *Countertop Ovens & Cook Surfaces utilize advancements in technology, materials & fabrication to design, create & engineer superior electrical appliances & devices needed to feed our families daily*

78. *I Will Now Show Good Faith Transparency and Full Disclosure in clearly pointing out the one & only thing a full-size electric range can do better than a countertop oven....*

79. *And That Is Cooking a Full-Sized Danged Turkey! & Danged Sides!... At the Same Danged Time!*

80. *And That Is IT!!!.... Other Than TURKEY Day your counter-top oven & countertop cook surface will absolutely run circles around your full-size electric range stove.... every day of the week.... every week of the month... every month of the year... forever & ever & ever.... promise...There is no way to compare them; however, i will try below.*

81. *It's Literally Jetsons VS Flintstones.... and the Flintstones showed two (2) hours late hung over with wicked explosive intestinal ail-ments....and no shoes on....*

82. *That Is Exactly How Worthless Your Primitive full-sized electric range oven is when producing the intense heat needed to feed you and your family every single day of your life....*

83. *EIGHT (8) AMPS IS A HUGE REDUCTION OF 47-AMPS... your countertop oven has very small Heating Elements that only require one leg of power to produce heat.*

84. *TEENY TINY HEATING KITS THAT CONSUME ONLY ONE LEG OF VOLTAGE Are Incapable ofHigh Amp Draws*

85. *YOUR FAMILY WINS The Moment You Plug in your 120-Volt Countertop oven as you will never spend food money on power-bill money ever ever again.*

86. *WHEN RENTERS AND HOMEOWNERS USE 120-VOLTS TO COOK THEY ARE:*

    a. *ESTABLISHING ENERGY consumption boundaries to feed their families*

    b. *REDUCING ENERGY consumption by eighty (80) percent when cooking on day one (1)*

    c. *TAKING STEPS TO Never Pay five (5) Dollars in Energy Cost to heat up two (2) dollars of food*

    d. *PROTECTING THEMSELVES from excessive unnecessary amp draw multiple times a day all year long*

87. *THE OSTER COUNTERTOP CONVECTION OVEN is extremely spacious. This is the perfect size for very large families. you can easily cook anything and everything inside…except a full size turkey and sides*

88. *SMALLER FAMILIES couples, & singles can purchase a medium to small size countertop convection oven that will not take up precious counter space in tiny homes/apartments*

89. *BIGGER IS NOT BETTER, DO NOT purchase a large countertop oven Or large countertop cook surface based on good looks and great reviews, purchase the smallest one you think is way too small…. if you find you need a larger countertop oven… you can always upgrade your current or even return it within 30 days…*

90. *WE ARE CHASING THE physically smallest countertop oven that will work for you and your family…*

91. *SMALLER COUNTERTOP OVEN AND COOKTOPS shopping is kinda like how we take our porridge…. One oven is way too small…. another may be way too big…..you just keep looking till you find the countertop oven that fits just right….*

92. *SMALLER COUNTERTOP OVEN AND COOKTOPS have smaller Heating Elements that require only one (1) line of voltage as they produce less amp draw while performing work*

93. *THE THIRTY-SIX ($36) DOLLAR small countertop oven at Walmart will provide sufficient heat to cook your tiny hot pockets, small frozen burritos, & single bologna slices all year long at the lowest amps. In time you will be able to buy more food to*

cook as your energy consumption cost drops through the floor. It takes a typical sixty (60) consecutive days to see the intense savings on the powerbill.

94. *MOST IMPORTANTLY.... Using a countertop oven/cook surfaces will consume 80% less energy than your full-size electric range oven.*

95. *IF YOU ARE SERIOUS ABOUT REDUCING YOUR your energy consumption, the only thing that should ever be cooked in your full-size electric range oven is a dang turkey.*

96. *<u>NEVER NEVER NEVER</u> store anything inside that would not survive your electric full-size range oven being accidentally turned on by visiting friends and family.*

97. *WE ARE NOW ARE NOW BAKING & COOKING at a fifth(5th) the excessive amp-draw of the full-size electric range.*

98. *THE METER IS now spinning five (5x) times slower when we bake all year long kettles, seek the smallest countertop cook surfaces to further reduce the energy consumption required to feed your family*

99. *DO NOT GET GREEDY our kitchen countertop receptacles have <u>amp</u> draw limitations*

100. *THROUGH NATIONWIDE UNIFORMITYevery Single-Family/ multi-family home nationwide have uniformity in the safety rating for wires that travel from the breaker boxes thru the walls in your home to land at receptacles*

101. *SINGLE FAMILY AND MULTI FAMILY HOMES HAVE A TYPICAL TWENTY (20A) AMP MAX for the electrical appliances & devices that are plugged into the kitchen countertop receptacles....*

102. *THAT SIMPLY MEANS IF ALL ELECTRICAL kitchen counter-top appliances are performing work at the same time and their combined amp draw exceeds 20 amps…. the 20-amp protection kitchen breaker would snap, removing voltage from every electrical device and appliances instantly….*

103. *That Simply Means THAT The Combined amp draw of all the electrical appliances & devices plugged into the kitchen counter receptacles exceeded twenty (20) amps total and the twenty (20) amp protection breaker snapped for safety.*

104. *The Twenty (20) Amp Protection Breaker Snapped when it detected more than twenty (20) amps traveling in the wires that are rated to carry only twenty (20) amp*

105. *THE BREAKER Snapped to Protect the Wire in the WALL before the wire destroys itself with the excessive amp draw over twenty (20) amps*

106. *KITCHEN PROTECTION BREAKER Snapped Because:*
    a. *SOMEBODY IN THE Kitchen got GREEDY…*
    b. *TOO MANY ELECTRICAL APPLIANCES AND DEVICES PERFORMING WORK IN THE KITCHEN at the same time*
    c. *TOO MANY ELECTRICAL APPLIANCES AND DEVICES in the kITCHEN WERE PERFORMING WORK & PRODUCING small individual amps-DRAWS that were slowly adding up*
    d. *COMBINED AMP DRAW exceeded twenty (20-A)amps*

107. *BREAKERS ARE SAFETY DEVICES RATED TO MATCH THE SAFETY SPECIFICATION OF THE OF THE Wire in the Wall, namely…. the thickness or gauge of the wire itself….*

108. *A 20-AMP BREAKER IS A SAFETY DEVICE RATED TO PROTECT A CERTAIN WIRE IN THE WALL THAT CANNOT*

CARRY MORE THAN TWENTY(20) Amp Breaker is a Safety Device Rated to Protect a Certain Size Sire in the Wall that cannot carry more than twenty (20-A)

109. *IF THE BREAKER DIDN'T SNAP, THE EXCESSIVE AMPS OVER TWENTY (20) would have destroyed the wire in the wall... with intense heat in matter of seconds.... from one side of the wire to the other*

110. *THREE (3) SECONDS BEFORE THE BEAKER SNAPPED. Amp draw from the kitchen appliances had Slowly been Slowly Creeping up Towards 20 amps For Quite Some Time Now....*

111. *IF THE BREAKER DIDN'T SNAP, THE EXCESSIVE AMPS OVER TWENTY (20) would have destroyed the wire in the wall... with intense heat in until the wires cannot provide voltage because they are burnt away into smithereens*

112. *THREE (3) SECONDS BEFORE THE BEAKER SNAPPEDAmp draw from the kitchen appliances had Slowly been Slowly Creeping up Towards 20 amps*

113. *LET'S LOOK AT THIS KITCHENS ELECTRICAL APPLIANCES THAT ARE ABOUT TO FORCE THE 20-AMP BREAKER to SNAP off as it protects the wire that carries the voltage from the breaker panel to the to the kitchen countertop receptacles*

114. *(5) SECONDS before kitchen breaker SNAPS*
    a. *A small countertop oven is consuming One Leg of Voltage to produce heat with a teeny tiny heating element. countertop oven is producing intense heat as the biscuits are almost done cooking..all while producing a typical 5.2 amps*
    b. *Small oven typical amp draw = 5.2 amps*
    c. *Total kitchen amp draw = 5.2 amps*

115. *(5) SECONDS before kitchen breaker SNAPS*

   a. *A small countertop cook surface is consuming 1 leg of voltage to make pancakes & bacon…this counter top cook surface has very small heating elements …Work is being performed as small griddle is producing a typical 5.3 amps*

   b. *Small cook surface typical amp draw = 5.3 amps*

   c. *Total kitchen amp draw =10.5 amps*

   d. *(4) SECONDS REMAIN before kitchen breaker SNAPS*

116. *(4) SECONDS before kitchen breaker SNAPS*

   a. *A light switch is turned on, a teeny tiny heating element in the form of a tungsten filament inside the light bulb is consuming one (1) leg of voltage & producing heat to illuminate the kitchen, The miniature heating element produces a typical 1.1 amps*

   b. *Light fixture typical amp draw = 1.1 amps*

   c. *Total kitchen amp draw = 11.6. amps*

117. *(4) SECONDS before kitchen breaker SNAPS*

   a. *The small kitchen fridge just completed an OFF cycle. The small compressor and small fan inside the fridge begin to perform work, fridge now cools drawing a typical 4.2 amps*

   b. *Small fridge typical amp draw = 4.2 amps*

   c. *Total kitchen amp draw = 15.8 amps*

   d. *(3) SECONDS now REMAIN before breaker SNAPS*

118. *(3) SECONDS Before kitchen breaker SNAPS*

   a. *A small circular fan on the kitchen counter is turned on. A mechanical motor begins consuming one (1) leg of voltage as it spins producing a typical 1.3 amps*

   b. *Small fan typical amp draw = 1.3 amps*

   c. *Total kitchen amp draw = 16.1 amps*

119. <u>*(3) SECONDS*</u> *Before kitchen breaker SNAPS*

    a. *A small T.V. on the kitchen countertop is turned on to check the weather report…. One leg of voltage is consumed as the T.V. screen displays reports of high humidity, and afternoon scattered showers all whilst producing a typical 1.2 amps*

    b. *Small T.V. typical amp draw = 1.2 amps*

    c. *Total kitchen amp draw = 17.3 amps*

    d. <u>*(2) SECONDS now REMAIN* </u> *before kitchen breaker SNAPS*

120. <u>*(2) SECONDS* </u> *Before kitchen breaker SNAPS*

    a. *A small radio on the kitchen counter is turned on and begins consuming one (1) leg of voltage to commence playing R & B songs producing a typical 0.8 amps*

    b. *Small radio typical amp draw = 0.8 amps*

    c. *Total kitchen amp draw = 18.1 amps*

121. <u>*(1) SECOND now REMAINs* </u> *before kitchen breaker SNAPS*

    a. *HERE comes the GREEEEEED as* <u>*FINALLY ONE (1) SECOND BEFORE THE BREAKER SNAPS:*</u>

    b. *The* **small** *blender on the kitchen counter is started to make a low calorie banana & strawberry smoothie. The small blender consumes one (1) leg of voltage & begins to spin the blender motor producing a typical 3.6 amps*

    c. *small blender typical amp draw = 3.6 amps*

    d. *Total kitchen amp draw =* <u>*21.7 amps*</u>

    e. <u>*NOW the 20-amp protection breaker SNAPS!!!!*</u>

122. *THE BREAKER SNAPS the instant the blender attempted to spin because the breakers in our homes ARE:*

a. *SAFETY DEVICES designed to protect wires in your walls from too much amp draw burning the wires into pieces and your home down to the foundation*

b. *NOT DESIGNED to protect your electrical appliances and electrical devices*

c. *NEVER NEVER NEVER to be UPSIZED, meaning a larger rated breaker is installed…*

d. *NEVER NEVER NEVER be REPLACED BY YOU or any other human Other Than: <u>A STATE LICENSED ELECTRICAL CONTRACTOR/ELECTRICIAN</u>*

e. *<u>EXACTLY IDENTICAL IN EVERY</u> single-family and multi-family residence in the entire United States (zinsco slimline included)*

f. *RATED TO MATCH AND PROTECT wires in walls*

g. *CONSIDERED A SINGLE POLE BREAKER if they protect a circuit containing only a single leg of voltage (receptacles)*

h. *CONSIDERED A DOUBLE POLE BREAKER if they protect a circuit containing both legs of voltage 240V*

123. *THE BREAKERS IN OUR MAIN PANEL ARE PROTECTION DEVICES…..THAT ARE RATED TO PROTECT THE PHYSICAL WIRE THAT CARRIES VOLTAGE….. .FROM MAIN PANEL TO THE KITCHEN..*

124. *EVERY SINGLE-FAMILY HOME KITCHEN AND MULTI-FAMILY KITCHEN TYPICALLY….HAVE A 20 AMP BREAKER PROTECTING THE WIRE THAT CARRIES VOLTAGE REQUIRED BY EVERY ELECTRICAL APPLIANCE & DEVICE IN THE KITCHIN…*

125. *BREAKERS IN YOUR HOME PROVIDE VOLTAGE THRU WIRES….& ALSO PROTECT WIRES FROM THE AMP DRAWS*

THAT ARE PULLED THRU SAME.....WIRES THAT PROVIDED VOLTAGE TO THE KITCHEN.....

126. *BREAKERS IN YOUR RATED TO PROTECT WIRES FROM AMP DRAW, FOR THIS REASON..... <u>YOU WILL NEVER NEVER NEVER NEVER REPLACE OR UPSIZE A BREAKER THAT KEEPS SNAPPING & SNAPPING & SNAPPING OVER AND OVER AND OVER AGAIN.</u>*

127. *YOU WILL NEVER NEVER NEVER NEVER ....<u>.....REPLACE OR UPSIZE A BREAKER IN YOUR LIFE EVER... EVER... EVER... EVER...</u>*

128. *<u>20-AMP MAX LIMITS EVERY U.S. KITCHEN DOWN TO ONLY ONE (1) COUNTERTOP OVEN AND ONLY ONE (1) SMALL COUNTERTOP COOK SURFACE AND THAT IS IT.... READ THAT AGIAN</u>*

129. *Through the: The Simple Art of Reducing Energy Consumption - The Definitive Guide- You successfully:*

    a. *Used your newly absorbed amp draw fundamentals to connect high excessive amp draw to your harmless looking Electric Range Oven.*

    b. *Learned you waste eighty (80%)percent of energy consumed to heat up your 240 volt full-size electric range for any small food that can be cooked in a 120 volt small counter top oven at a fifth (5ᵗʰ) of the energy consumption.*

    c. *Retained knowledge your family will lose every time you cook anything except a turkey in your electric range oven*

    d. *Identified electrical fundamentals that explain why & how breakers protect wires in walls from excessive over-amp-draw that will burn wires*

e. *Chosen to protect your family and home by never replacing or upsizing a breaker that is snapping & snapping & snapping over and over again.*

f. *Committed to the safety of your family and home by NEVER letting any carbon-based life form replace a breaker in your home Other Than A State Licensed Electrical Contractor*

g. *Established your electric range oven is the highest amp draw produced with its typical 47 amp draw*

h. *Classified your home as either single-family house with neighbors that (DO NOT share walls) OR Multi-family house that (DOES HAVE) neighbors that share walls*

i. *Forced your spinning meter to spin five (5X) times slower cook and bake for your family every single minute/ hour/ day/ week/ month of the entire year because you are now cooking while consuming one (1) leg of voltage (120 Volts) with a typical 8 amps of a countertop oven/cooksurface INSTEAD OF consuming both legs of voltage (240 Volts) and a heinous typical 47 amp draw of your full-size electric range oven.*

j. *On your path to start paying two (2) dollars in energy to heat up five(5) dollars worth food in about sixty(60) after you have shown discipline and your power bills are now a small FRACTION of the two(2) , three (3) and even four-hundred ($400) dollar monthly power bills that are currently EATING YOU & YOUR FAMILY ALIVE*

130. *BRAVO What a Great Start In Our Noble Quest to Destroy Our Predictable Routine High Power Bills With Extreme Prejudice And Absolute Accuracy...*

131. *You have learned so much about your home in just our short time together...Your oven can never starve you and your family ever again,* **You will never pay good money to purchase expensive energy, then waste 80% of it.... and your power box is looking less and less mysterious by the minute....** *and that was just STEP ONE....Lets move on :)*

STEP TWO(2)

WHICH HOME APPLIANCE PRODUCES THE SINGLE LARGEST AMp DRAW OVER THE ENTIRE YEAR? WHICH APPLIANCE STEALS FROM US? WHICH ELECTRICAL APPLIANCE IS STEADY TAKING YOUR MONEY AND GIVING YOU ABSOLUTELY NOTHING IN RETURN

Lets Talk

HOT WATER

"KNOW THY ENEMY"   Sun Tzu - The Art of War

132. *Electrical Appliances That produce heat produce the highest amp draw.*

133. *Electrical Appliances That produce heat produce the highest amp draw.*

134. *ELECTRIC HOT WATER TANKS PRODUCE THE HIGHEST AMP DRAW OVER <u>THE ENTIRE YEAR</u>*

135. *<u>The Simple Art of Reducing Energy Consumption -The Definitive Guide-</u> TARGETS YOUR ELECTRIC HOT WATER TANK WITH SUSPICION, CONTEMPT, & WELL DEFINED PROTOCOLS*

136. *Dominating Your Electric Hot Water Tank is crucial in reducing your home's yearly energy consumption,We Start Now.*

137. *We Consume Disturbing Amounts of energy heating the water in our homes. This is because electric hot water tanks TYPICALLY:*
    a. *Consume Both Legs of voltage/240-VOLTS to perform work*
    b. *Mass Produced with two (2) large heating elements & two (2) adjustable internal thermostats*
    c. *Produce a Typical 26 amp draw that keeps that meter spinning like a top*
    d. *Represent Fifty <u>(50%)</u> Percent of our homes' energy consumption over the entire year*
    e. *Produce The Largest amp draw over the duration of the entire year.*
    f. *Intermittently Stay On All Year Long keeping our bathing water piping hot twenty-four(24) a day, seven(7) days a week, three hundred sixty five(365) days a year*

138. *SO HOW HOT IS YOUR HOT WATER HHHHHHHHMMMMMMMMM??*

139. *Go to Your Kitchen Sink, turn on the hot water & wait for 5 minutes.*

140. *Do You See STEAM?*

141. *Do You Have to Mix Cold Water with Hot Water to Avoid Scalding showers?*

142. *If You Answered YES to these questions your Electric Hot Water Tank is Set Too High!!!*

143. *HOT WATER THAT IS PRODUCING STEAM AT YOUR FAUCETS ALWAYS CONSUMES EXPENSIVE COLOSSAL AMOUNTS OF ENERGY HOURLY!!!*

144. *When You See Steam Or are forced to to mix cold water to avoid burning showers YOU ARE:*

    a. *Consuming Obscene Amounts of very very very expensive energy every single minute of every single day all year long for nothing.*

    b. *Producing an Excessive Amp Draw every minute/hour/week/month all year long for nothing to show for it.*

    c. *Keeping Your Meter Spinning Faster all year long for absolutely nothing.*

    d. *Paying One Hundred Twenty Dollars($120) Extra on top of your already high monthly power bill every month of the year for nothing*

    e. *Feeding Your Hot Water Tank both legs of Voltage before you feed your family for nothing in return.*

    f. *Wasting Energy for Nothing at all.*

    g. *Forcing High Power Bills on yourself*

145. *If You Live In An Apartment or Rental Property We will wait a quick minute while you call the leasing office & put in a maintenance request to have your electric hot water tank temperature turned down immediately.... Your Back! You Look Happy-I love it! lets keep going:)*

146. *Every Typical Electrical Hot Water Tank contains the same two universal thermostats & two heating elements.*

147. *If You Get "5 minutes" of Hot Water one of your heating elements has failed and needs to be replaced A.S.A.P.*

148. *Electric Hot Water Tank's two (2) Internal thermostats TYPICALLY:*
    a. *Are Turned Up by the previous renters and or homeowners.*
    b. *Have a Max Temp of 160 degrees.*
    c. *Have a Min Temp of 120 degrees.*
    d. *Are Factory Set for 130 degrees*

149. *JUST THINK ABOUT IT…. YOUR ELECTRIC HOT WATER TANK IS PIPING HOT TWENTY- FOUR (24) HOURS A DAY…. EVERY SINGLE DAY OF THE YEAR… DESPITE THE FACT YOU TYPICALLY TAKE ONE SHOWER A DAY ON AVERAGE….*

150. *What's the fix? Those internal thermostats must be tuned down A.S.A.P*

151. *Consult with A Licensed Plumber…. Be clear that you want to pay a service fee to "have your electric hot water tank turned down" nothing more.*

152. *I Cannot Advise You on The Temperature…. Mine are turned down to the minimum; however, I would happily take a decently warm quick bath in exchange for producing the absolute lowest amp draw all year long*

153. *Some Homes with lots of showers daily (kids) or routine baths may require temperatures closer to the factory setting.*

154. *Once The Plumbing Company Arrives, <u>SHOW THEM the Electric Hot Water Tank.</u> Upon Completion pay the pre-agreed price, reach for your pocket-book, hand him ($20) cash & then <u>SHOW THEM THE DOOR.</u>*

155. *That Twenty ($20) Dollar Bill Will come back to you one hundred-fold as the the electrical hot water tank is still producing its typical 23 amps; However, The Electric Hot Water Tank IS NOW:*
   a. *Primarily* Off
   b. *Primarily Not Consuming both legs of voltage (240V) to perform work.*
   c. *Not Energizing Large heating elements nearly every minute daily*
   d. *Producing an Amp Draw forty (40%) percent less the entire year.*
   e. *Forcing Your Meter Spin forty(40%) percent less during the entire year*

156. *Further Methodically Reduce the energy consumption of your electric hot water tank by ALWAYS:*
   a. *Washing Dishes in cold water*
   b. *Washing Clothes in cold water*

157. *In The Absence of Using hot water we must lean on chemical engineers that produce superior cold-water soaps THAT WILL:*
   a. *Clean Plates And Pans better than traditional hot water*
   b. *Not Ruin Plates by leaving stains & streaks over time.*

158. *THIS NEXT PART IS SPOOKY, YOUR OWN DISHWASHER IS PLOTTING AGAINST YOU….*

159. *Make Sure To Inspect the Buttons on Your dishwasher.*

160. *You May Have Buttons for either cold water, or hot water, select cold water.*

161. *While You're There look for a button that says "HEATED DRY"*

162. *Decent Newer Dishwashers have an electrical heating element that spends a typical sixteen(16) minutes drying your dishes whilst producing intense heat at a cheeky fourteen(14) amp draw…. and that spinning meter responds as it spins faster and harder*

163. *Get up Right Now and walk into your kitchen. Approach your dishwasher w/ disgust, repulsion & contempt in your eyes as you scan the button panel.*

164. *Found Them!? Yep! that's them, now do me a favor.*

165. *Extend Your Favorite Finger on your favorite hand AS YOU:*
    a. *Turn The The Drying button OFF*
    b. *Select The Cold water option*

166. *Turning OFF The Plate Drying Option is crucial in reducing your energy consumption….*

167. *I'm Certain We All Now Understand That electrical appliances that Produce Heat also produce the ……. … ….*

168. *ou Just Mentally Said The Highest Amp Draw :):):):) Now we are just plain having fun :):):):)*

169. *One Final Electrical Hot Water Tank tactical strategy to cut your current energy consumption in half Effective Immediately.*

170. *The Way to Consume the Lowest Amount of Energy to heat the water in your home all year long Is to leave the breaker for the electric hot water tank OFF all year long.*

171. *This Ultimate Reduction of Energy Consumption technique may not work for a home that has a high number of occupants or extensive daily showers.*

172. *Renters & Homeowners Will experience astronomically enormous reduction of energy consumption when they are disciplined enough to CONSISTENTLY:*

    a. *Turn The Hot Water Breaker ON 15 minutes prior to shower-time*

    b. *Turn The Hot Water Breaker OFF after shower-time*

173. *Small Homes & Apartments will have a decent likelihood of reaching the "double digit energy bill club" a.k.a (monthly power bills under $99 dollars) WHEN THEY:*
    a. *Diligently Practice In the Simple Art of Reducing Energy Consumption*
    b. *Turn The Electric Hot Tank ON only prior to shower*
    c. *Turn The Electric Hot Tank OFF after showertime*

174. *If This Is A Viable Option for your home, I advise using a Licensed Electrical Contractor to add a turn dial timer next to the electric hot water tank…. This Energy Reduction Modification WILL:*
    a. *Change The Structure of your home*
    b. *Require an Electrical Contractor To Pull a Permit with your local county.*

175. *Keep In Mind the electrical hot water tank produces a typical 26 amp draw as incredible Intense heat is produced.*

176. *The Heating Elements inside the tank get cherry red hot when the tank is on.*

177. *It Only Takes Fifteen(15) minutes to heat the tank full of water...*

178. *The Way to Identify Your electric hot water tank breaker is to take a hot shower, then turn everything off inside your home to make it as quiet as possible...*

179. *Put Your Ear Against your electric hot water tank, and you will "hear" a sizzling as the cherry red electrical heating elements are heating up the water...*

180. *Next Open Your Breaker Panel. Find the double pole (thick) breaker that is Typically rated thirty(30) amps in size.*

181. *Turn This Breaker OFF and put your ear back to the tank...*

182. *Once You Have Turned Off the correct breaker, the electric hot water tank will be silent or not sizzling as the electric heating elements are NOT heating up the water...*

183. *Don't Forget To Check for the sizzling sound after your hot shower...*

184. *The Hot Shower Ensures The Tank Will Be In An ON Position as the 240V electric heating elements are heating the cold water that is replacing the hot water you just consumed in the shower.*

185. *KEEP IN MIND THE ELECTRIC RANGE OVEN & ELECTRIC HOT WATER TANK CONSUME THE MOST ENERGY IN EVERY AMERICAN HOME*

186. *THIS IS BECAUSE THE ELECTRIC RANGE STOVE & ELECTRIC HOT WATER TANK PRODUCE THE MOST HEAT OVER THE ENTIRE YEAR*

187. *WITH OUR FIRST TWO (2) STEPS COMPLETE, WE CAN CLEARLY SEE THE 120-VOLT COUNTERTOP OVEN/COOK SURFACE AND CONTROLLED ELECTRIC HOT WATER TANK WORK FOR US NOW.... THEY CAN NEVER EVER HURT US AGAIN*

188. *Through The Simple Art of Reducing Energy Consumption -The Definitive Guide- WE HAVE*
    a. *Reduced Our Energy Consumption of an original excessive 47 amp draw down 8 amps when cooking*
    b. *Reduced Our Energy Consumption by eighty(80%) percent when we bake & cook multiple times a day.*

c. *Reduced Our Energy Consumption by commanding our meter to spin five(5)times slower when we cook*

d. *Reduced Our Energy Consumption by reducing or completely stopping the production of intense heat our electric hot water tanks produce*

e. *Reduced Our Energy Consumption by forcing our meter to spin forty (40%) percent less time as we heat our water over a lifetime.*

189. *With Two(2) Simple Lifestyle Changes to reduce your energy consumption you have also reduced the likelihood of ever receiving a monthly excessively high power bill ever ever ever ever ever again.*

190. *So Far So Good In Your Noble Effort to "save on the monthly power bill" it's nice to see you finally "saving power"....*

191. *TOO BAD WE ARE NOT here to learn how to "save on the power bill"....*

192. *Let Me Be Very Very Very Clear, I AM NOT HERE for "savings" and "discounts" on your "power bill".... I don't know any nifty coupon clipping tips and tricks....*

193. *I AM HERE TO TEACH YOU Complete Control & Total Absolute Domination of your Monthly Astronomical Power Bills...*

194. *With That Being Said, I will try once more to define what you are doing....*

195. *So Far So Good In Your Noble efforts to permanently reduce your energy consumption as YOU ARE NOW:*

a. *SETTING FIRM AND STRICT ENERGY CONSUMPTION BOUNDARIES WHILE*

b. DEMANDING TOTAL EFFICIENCY FROM YOUR ELECTRICAL 240-VOLT APPLIANCES THAT PRODUCE INTENSE HEAT

196. *See How Much More Accurate & sweet sounding my second attempt was? :)*

197. *Two(2) Steps Down, Two(2) To Go*

198. *Let us move on to our final home appliance that has the propensity to keep the electrical meter spinning fast all year long…. right beneath our noses….*

STEP THREE(3)

WHICH HOME APPLIANCE WASTE ENORMOUS AMOUNTS OF ENERGY ALL YEAR LONG WHICH APPLIANCE IS WASTING YOUR MONEY DAILY? WHICH ELECTRICAL APPLIANCE IS BY YOUR FAMILY TO ABUSE YOUR FAMILY EVERY SINGLE DAY?

Lets Talk

CORPORAL

PUNISHMENT

"KNOW THY ENEMY"

Sun Tzu - The Art of War

Have you figured out the final appliance in your home that produces heat and pulls the highest amp draw over the entire year?

199. *It is your (expletive expletive) CLOTHES DRYER!!! Typical dryer produces a typical 24 amp draw to dry your clothes!*

200. *MY FLORIDA HOMEOWNERS AND RENTERS BOP THEMSELVES UPSIDE THE HEAD WHEN THEY TOSS A FEW WET ITEMS INTO THE DRYER*

201. *Maybe a pair of work scrubs,*

202. *Maybe a favorite pair of jeans*

203. *Maybe a single item of clothing that is "wrinkled" & is put back into the dryer to "get the wrinkles out."*

204. *Sound familiar? If you have lots of family and or specifically teenagers in your home, chances are that The dryer is used year round to dry a few articles of clothing.*

205. *This is an excessive & unnecessary consumption of extremely expensive energy all danged year long!*

206. *Ooohhhhh and how the Meter spins with intent and purpose as the dryer produces 24 amps producing intense heat required TO DRY A SINGLE HOODIE:*

    a. every single morning

    b. every day of the week before school

    c. and more on the weekends!!!

207. *Consult with a dryer vent company Immediately that exclusively does dryer vent cleaning.*

208. *Stay away from dryer vent companies that also do "alleged" air conditioning duct cleanings.*

209. *Removing that lint build up every single year inside of the dryer vent is absolutely crucial to reducing your homes energy consumption*

210. *Keeping your dryer vent clean reduces energy consumption because a clean dryer vent equates to:*
    a. *faster dry times*
    b. *not having to dry damp clothes for two complete cycles (double (2x) bop to the head)*

211. *Calmly sit your teenage children down and tell them that you:*
    a. *are shocked, deeply disturbed & overall flabbergasted with their habitual reckless energy consumption.*
    b. *have replaced the passage door knob (no lock) utility room with a entry door knob (has lock)*

212. *take your time as you gently explain to them that MOVING FORWARD:*
    a. *Using the Washer and Dryer for a single article of clothing will be viewed as mutiny and will be dealt with in a medieval fashion.*
    b. *The door to the utility room will be unlocked on Saturday for six(6) hours...and that's it.*
    c. *The dryer will never be turned on unless it is full of clothes.*
    d. *cold water will now be used for clothes & dishes*

213. *After you have explained the paragraph above BE SURE TO MAKE THEM:*
    a. *write the above mentioned paragraph down on a piece of paper.*
    b. *read the above mentioned paragraph quietly to themselves twice*
    c. *recite the above mentioned paragraph three(3x) times.... loud enough for the neighbors to hear.*

214. *Leave a brand new never-before seen single flip flop on the table during this discussion...*

215. *The flip flop is demonstrative evidence that firmly yet subtly sets the tone while establishing definitive consequences and repercussions.*

216. *If the new ring camera you place in the laundry room ever suggests all three(3) teenagers insist on tossing their favorite pair of jeans/hoodies into the dryer every morning, then by all means consult with your flip flop for viable teenager reprogramming.*

217. *let's think about this logically, You are literally losing money by not using the flip flop as needed.*

218. *If using a flip flop to occasionally motivate your teenagers is not your style...*

219. *Well then fair enough. For you I suggest placing a plastic jar on top of the dryer...*

220. *Moving forward each teenager will place four ($4) dollars into the jar when they want to simply "use the dryer" before school to "get wrinkles out"*

221. *It's 6 dollars in the jar if they have the audacity to use the washer & dyer in combination to clean a a few items of clothing.*

222. Oddly enough I imagine most teenagers would rather keep the money & take the flip flop beating instead...in that case i advise a thicker flip flop.

223. I urge you to not settle for less than beatings or cold hard cash in the jar....

224. The teens will learn either discipline & crucial impulse control, or fair-trade concepts & contributions in achieving sustainable development.

225. And in turn, the electrical meter spins slower & slower & slower as the year progresses...oh my!

226. Last clothes dryer techniques for reducing the daily energy consumption required to clean and dry our clothes all year long.

227. If you have a large family you naturally must wash and dry an obscene amount of clothes weekly.

228. 233. I suggest you wash your three(3) loads at home then take damp clothes to a local, safe, indoor, video monitored coin-op laundry to dry your clothes.

229. LOCAL COIN-OP LAUNDROMATS TYPICALLY HAVE BIG COMMERCIAL DRYERS THAT DRY YOUR THREE (3) DAMP LOADS ALL AT ONCE FOR SIX (6) QUARTERS

230. Drying three(3) loads of wet clothes is another excessive, & unnecessary consumption of extremely expensive energy.

231. When we dry our clothes at home instead of a local Coin-Op laundry we will lose every time because drying three(3) damp loads at home will always:

    a. require a dry time close to 2 hours.

    b. produce an excessive 24 amp draw

    c. command our meter to spin spin spin

232. Or.... take your three damp loads, six(6) quarters and your wall charger to your local coin op laundry...

233. Drying three(3) loads at your local coin op laundromat will typically cost you:

    a. six(6) quarters

    b. your time

    c. some patience....

234. Drying three(3) loads in your home will cost you sixteen($16) dollars and that is a serious underestimate....

235. Sixteen($16) dollars is three(3) gallons of milk and two(2) loaves of bread and a milky way bar....lets act accordingly here.

236. Final clothes dryer technique, <u>Many many years ago</u>, power companies would charge half price per kilowatt hour for energy consumption that occurs between midnight and six(6am)

237. These off hours are discounted considering the majority of Americans are asleep between midnight and six(6AM)

238. This discounted price per kilowatt hour during the Off peak hours may still be in place, or it may have been stopped years ago, consult with your local power company to confirm.

239. If the off-peak discount per kilowatt hour is still offered to its customers, then this is the absolute perfect time to:

    a. start the large damp load in the dryer

    b. start the fully loaded dishwasher

    c. start the timer on your slow-cooker pot

    d. spin that turn dial next to the electric hot water tank

240. Now you are fully engaged in <u>The Simple Art of Reducing Energy Consumption</u> as you produce intense heat in your home at half price during off peak hours....(expletive)yassss:)))

241. *And the electrical meter responds by spinning slower and slower and slower and slower and slower and slower and slower and slower all year long....*

242. *Final Amp Draw Reference*
   a. *oven range typically 47 amps*
   b. *Hot water tank typically 24 amps*
   c. *Clothes dryer typically 24 amps*
   d. *240 volt jacuzzi typically 34 amps*
   e. *Amish fireplaces sold on tv typically 18 amps*
   f. *5 ton residential AC system typically 15 amps*
   g. *Hair dryer typically 13 amps*
   h. *3 ton residential AC system typically 11 amps*
   i. *1.5 ton residential AC system typically 8 amps*
   j. *Blender typically 4 amps*
   k. *Vacuum typically 3 amps*
   l. *Ceiling fan typically 2 amps*
   m. *60 watt light bulb typically 1 amp*
   n. *Xbox typically 1 amp*

243. *As an air conditioning contractor.... Imagine how I feel when the world believes heating and cooling are fifty(50%) percent of your home's energy consumption.*

244. *Now that you understand amp draw... please notice that typical residential A/C system amp draws are between 8 amps to 16 amps all depending on the tonnage of the system.*

245. *This entire definitive guide began on our around 5/22/23 in a local facebook community group...*

246. *A homeowner made a post about her high power bills inasmuch as seeking referrals for new siding and attic insulation....*

247. *The comments in the post were so far beyond wrong, I knew I had to set the record straight....immediately.*

248. *I started this guide to object to the errant status quo.*

249. *I wish to educate/teach/inspire my treasured/cherished/precious Florida renters and homeowners.*

250. *I can testify to my beloved Florida homeowners who are about to lose their marbles because they've already replaced the entire AC system, ductwork, siding and attic insulation... and still... The monthly power bill remains absurdly astronomical.*

251. *My Floridians trying hard and <u>still losing</u> was the incendiary impulse of inception essential to/commence/ focus/ execute/ this definitive guide.*

252. *I have spent the last 30 days-straight formatting and streamlining this publication by the minute/day/ week.*

253. *It's been a beautiful whirlwind of cascading blessings and absolute high favor....thank you universe... I am grateful...*

254. *This publication is created in love to be shared in richest/simple/email so it can be shared without a download, or link or attachment.*

255. *Just one email ready for mass communication.....*

256. *And in time and with enough elbow grease ...perhaps the beautiful sophistication of a proper hardback publication infused with the glorious legacy of a highly coveted goliath publishing house... .*

257. *I graduated from Tampa Bay tech-high school class of 1999 with a degree in heating ventilation and air conditioning. H.V.A.C*

258. *One of the first theories we learned was amp draw consumption.*

259. *From 2001 to 2013 I worked for apartment complexes as a maintenance tech, then eventually as a maintenance supervisor for the final 10 years.*

260. *This is how I have such extensive knowledge of all residential appliances, troubleshooting, and many construction trade aspects....*

261. *What I have just shared with you I was sharing with my beloved tenants in the apartment complexes I worked at 20 plus years ago....*

262. *In 2013, I left the apartment complex industry to focus on working for other air conditioning contractors, so I could one day open my own air conditioning company...*

263. *In February 2017, I earned my air conditioning contractor's license finally achieving the dream of opening my own air conditioning company.*

264. *In March of 2022 I was forced into unforeseen early retirement to become a full time pro se litigant in my high conflict three (3) year long paternity action...*

265. *My character building situation last year that forced my early retirement has been brilliantly ameliorated through kindness, compassion, commitment, focus, and sheer will.... Learning how to draft legal motions in linear fashion is what made this publication possible.*

266. *This publication winds down now with accurate techniques to minimize the energy consumption of your central home air conditioning system.*

267. *Yeah I know my stuff with the above-mentioned techniques that reduce energy consumption and excessive amp draw all day long.......*

268......*However, when it comes to residential air-conditioning in applications under five(5) tons, I could/can and will literally write the book....*

269. *We now close step three(3) with a proper flash examination of the simple three(3) energy reduction lifestyle changes we have learned together thus far.*

270. *Naturally it seems like we are just making a few semi-intrusive, inconvenient simple changes that may just seem silly or maybe not make sense at all.... And that's ok, Folks may criticize/question/laugh... And that's ok too, I promise.... That's how you know you are doing it right:)*

271. *Congratulations.... Step Three(3) Complete.... You now seek dominance over the electrical appliances that produce intense heat in your home every day of the year.:)*

272. *You will Never Ever Ever Engage in the simple energy consumption blunders that are soooo easy for all carbon based lifeforms to make:)*

273. *Moving forward...refer to your step 3 reference sheet below when explaining to your family why these semi-intrusive & inconvenient simple changes that may just seem silly or maybe not make sense at all <u>ARE NOW standing daily protocol & procedures.... effective immediately.... YES LIKE TODAY</u>*

274. *Moving forward... refer to your step(3) reference below when others poke and laugh and say you're dumb as you embark on your first 60 days with methodical simple energy consumption reduction hard protocols in place.*

275. <u>Through</u> **<u>The Simple Art of Reducing Energy Consumption -The Definitive Guide-</u>** <u>YOU HAVE NOW EFFECTIVELY:</u>

    a. <u>PERFECTLY PLACED THE HEEL OF YOUR BOOT OF THE TRACHEA</u> *of the electric range oven that's been eating you alive with its flagrant daily cryptic (hidden), abusive, repeated, routine excessive daily/ weekly/yearly high amp draws*

    b. <u>SLIPPED A BLADE BETWEEN THE FIFTH (5TH) & SIXTH (6TH) RIBS</u> *precisely puncturing the liver of the electric hot water tank that's been burning you alive with its cryptic nonstop hourly high amp draw.*

    c. <u>PLACED AN INCENDIARY DEVISE ON THE UNDERCARRIAGE</u> *of the electric dryer that's been frolicing as it slowly torches your hard earned savings with regular routine rampant excessive HIGH AMP DRAW*

276. <u>*I AM FULL OF JOY AND GRATITUDE AS THE UNIVERSE GIVES ME FRONT ROW SEAT AND TEENY TINY BINOCULARS TO OBSERVE YOU*</u> **Inflict absolute control over the excessive amp draw of your everyday electrical appliances that were inflicting financial pain upon you & your family...**

277. <u>*I AM SO GRATEFUL TO THE UNIVERSE ON LEVELS YOU CAN'T FATHOM WHEN I CLOSE MY EYES AND ALL I SEE IS*</u> **My U.S. homeowners/renters all beginning to share their sixty 60 day high power bill butchering stories w/ POWER, PRIDE & CONFIDENCE**

278. <u>*I SEEK INEVITABLE CONCURRED CONFIRMED & BONAFIDE REPORTS OF RENEWED VIGOR SPREADING LIKE HOTCAKES*</u> **...Hotcakes that happened to be cooked on your recently acquired 120V countertop skillet cook surface at a**

fraction of the amp draw of your malevolent full size ELECTRIC RANGE OVEN....

279. <u>*LAST ONE... I NEED FRESH ICED COFFEE, TWO (2) POTASSIUM RICH BANANAS & AN EXTRA NITROGLYCERIN TABLET TO SIMMER THE EXCITEMENT AS I DRIFT OFF WITH*</u> *sweet visions of renters and homeowners walking up to their own major electrical appliances as they kick it once, and scream, "IT WAS YOU!!! IT WAS YOU THE WHOLE TIME!!!"*

280. <u>*I TOLD YOU I AM NOT HERE TO HELP YOU*</u> *clip coupons and hunt bargains....*

281. <u>*I TOLD YOU I AM HERE TO TEACH YOU HOW TO*</u> *dominate your power bills with EXTREME PREJUDICE AND ABSOLUTE ACCURACY ABOVE ALL*

282. <u>*THREE (3) STEPS DOWN ONE(1) STEP TO GO,*</u> *Damn fine work so far to all you; however, we are not done yet, WE STILL HAVE, "THINGS LEFT TO DO"....*

283. *.....END STEP THREE....*

STEP FOUR(4)

WHICH HOME APPLIANCE IS NEGLECTED ABUSED AND BETRAYED DAILY? WHICH APPLIANCE KEEPS YOUR METER SPINNING WHEN NEGLECTED? WHICH ELECTRICAL APPLIANCE WASTE YOUR MONEY WHEN ABUSED BY YOU

Let's Talk

H.V.A.C. NEGLECT ABUSE AND BETRAYAL

"KNOW THY ENEMY"
Sun Tzu - The Art of War

284. *FIRST THINGS FIRST, I AM ABOUT TO THE SAME THING IN ELEVEN (11) different fonts to make sure it sinks in.... heads up now, THIS WILL BE ON THE MIDTERM...*

285. *YOU ARE USING THE WRONG AIR FILTER, you are using the wrong air filter, YOU ARE USING THE WRONG AIR FILTER, you are using the wrong air filter, YOU ARE USING THE WRONG AIR FILTER, you are using the wrong air filter, YOU ARE USING THE WRONG AIR FILTER, you are using the wrong air filter, YOU ARE USING THE WRONG AIR FILTER, you are using the wrong air filter, YOU ARE USING THE WRONG AIR FILTER, you are using the wrong air filter, YOU ARE USING THE WRONG AIR FILTER, YOU ARE USING THE WRONG AIR FILTER*

286. *FIVE (5) EASY QUICK CONCEPTS EARS UP, EYES OPEN, CAN'T LOSE THE PROFESSOR IS IN, WE START WITH:*

    a. NATIONWIDE UNIFORMITY IN CENTRAL H.V.A.C SYSTEM RESIDENTIAL APPLICATIONS IN FIVE (5) TONS AND UNDER

    b. FIBERGLASS FILTER VS PLEATED FILTER & HOW DAILY AMP DRAW IS AFFLICTED...

    c. BI-ANNUAL MAINTENANCE & HOW AMP DRAW IS AT STAKE

    d. CORRECTING AIR IMBALANCES IN YOUR HOME & HOW HOURLY AMP DRAW IS INCREASED

    e. THE TOP FIVE (5) NATIONAL BRANDS AND HOW LONG- TERM AMP DRAW IS IMPACTED.

287. *NATURALLY WE START AGAIN WITH NATIONWIDE UNIFORMITY....THUS, OUR H.V.A.C LESSON BEGINS WITH THE VERY ACRONYM* "....H.V.A.C...." *IT STANDS FOR HEATING, VENTILATION, AND AIR- CONDITIONING, EACH WORD IS CRUCIAL AND HAS DIRECT IMPACT ON AMP DRAW*

288. *IT MUST BE KNOWN THAT U.S. RESIDENTIAL H.V.A.C SYSTEMS ARE DEFINED AND CLASSIFIED BY THE WAY THEY PRODUCE HEAT FOR THE HOME THEREFORE, OUR ACRONYM* "H.V.A.C" *BEGINS WITH THE WORD* "... HEATING..."

289. *U.S. MULTI-FAMILY/SINGLE-FAMILY HOMES ARE TYPICALLY BUILT WITH EITHER A (120V) VOLT COMBUSTION FURNACE(GAS/OIL/PROPANE) OR (240V) ELECTRIC FURNACE (HEATING ELEMENT)*

290. *IN MY NATIVE FLORIDA, AND EXTREMELY SOUTHERN REGIONS, THE ELECTRIC FURNACE EQUIPPED WITH HEATING ELEMENTS IS KING, THE REST OF THE NATION BELONGS TO THE COMBUSTION FURNACE DESIGNED TO BURN (COMBUST) NATURAL OIL*

291. *OUR SECOND WORD OF OUR* "...H.V.A.C..." *ACRONYM BELONGS TO* "...VENTILATION..." *EASILY DEFINED AS THE PROCESS OF EXCHANGING AIR IN ANY SPACE TO REMOVE MOISTURE*

292. *A HOMES FURNACE REGARDLESS OF ELECTRIC OR COMBUSTION IS BUILT FOR TWO THINGS.... PROVIDE HEAT FOR THE HOME, AND EXCHANGE THE AIR IN THE HOME AT LEAST SIX (6) TIMES PER HOUR*

293. *WE CLOSE OUR "H.V.A.C" ACRONYM WITH A.C, THAT BELONGS TO "AIR CONDITIONING" THAT IS A STRAIGHT COOL OR HEAT PUMP CONDENSER*

294. *NOW LET'S MAKE THIS SIMPLE WITH THE DISSECTION OF THE WORD "...CENTRAL SPLIT SYSTEM..."*

295. *REGARDLESS OF COMBUSTION OR ELECTRIC FURNACE, REGARDLESS OF HEAT PUMP OR STRAIGHT COOL CONDENSER, THINK "SPLIT SYSTEM"*

296. *THE WORD "...SPLIT SYSTEM..." SIMPLIFIES ONE MACHINE INSIDE THE HOME, AND ONE MACHINE OUTSIDE THE HOME, WITH BOTH MACHINES CONNECTED BY COPPER TUBING...*

297. *NOW FORGET ELECTRIC OR COMBUSTION FURNACE... INSTEAD SIMPLY SEE AN "... INDOOR MACHINE..."*

298. *NOW FORGET AIR CONDITIONING STRAIGHT COOL OR HEAT PUMP CONDENSER... INSTEAD SIMPLY SEE AN "... OUTDOOR MACHINE..."*

299. *THE INDOOR MACHINE WAS DESIGNED TO HEAT YOUR HOME AND ENSURE PROPER VENTILATION a.k.a (EXCHANGE/CIRCULATION) OF INDOOR AIR IN ANY RESIDENTIAL SPACE.*

300. *THIS MEANS EVERY INDOOR MACHINE IN THE U.S. MUST ABSOLUTELY EXCHANGE THE INDOOR AIR AT LEAST SIX (6X) TIMES PER HOUR FOR PROPER EFFICIENCY AND PERFORMANCE.... THIS IS EXACTLY WHAT "... VENTILATION..." PERTAINS TO IN RESIDENTIAL H.V.A.C.*

301. *THIS MEANS EVERY OUTDOOR MACHINE IS USES A MANDATORY (240V) ELECTRICAL COMPRESSOR TO MOVE ITS REFRIGERANT IN ONE DIRECTION IN A CONSTANT*

CYCLE BETWEEN THE INDOOR MACHINE AND OUTDOOR MACHINE USING THE TWO (2) COPPER LINES THAT CONNECT THEM.

302. *NOW LET'S CONNECT THE DOTS...* MULTI-FAMILY/ SINGLE FAMILY HOMES NATION WIDE TYPICALLY HAVE *AN H.V.A.C SPLIT SYSTEM STARRING AN INDOOR MACHINE THAT* PRODUCES HEAT AND IS RESPONSIBLE FOR *{EXCHANGING} THE INDOOR AIR SIX (6x) TIMES PER HOUR* IN THE NAME OF ADEQUATE VENTILATION.

303. *H.V.A.C SPLIT SYSTEMS IN AMERICAN HOMES HAVE AN OUTDOOR UNIT THAT CONSUMES BOTH LEGS OF VOLTAGE AS A 240V ELECTRICAL COMPONENT IN THE FORM OF A* REFRIGERANT COMPRESSOR CYCLES ITS REFRIGERANT IN CONSTANT LOOP BETWEEN THE INDOOR AND OUTDOOR MACHINE...

304. *ALL THIS TO SAY IS THE ONLY LETTER OF THE ACRONYM* THAT HOMEOWNERS & RENTERS CONTROL IS {... VENTILATION...}

305. *INFACT,* MAINTAINING ADEQUATE VENTILATION OVER THE LIFE *OF THE SPLIT SYSTEM FALLS DIRECTLY ON THE SHOULDERS OF* BOTH RENTERS AND HOMEOWNERS NATIONWIDE...

306. *H.V.A.C SYSTEMS LITERALLY LIVE OR DIE* DEPENDING ON ADEQUATE VENTILATION

307. *HOMEOWNERS AND RENTERS FORCE THEIR OWN H.V.A.C SYSTEMS* TO PRODUCE AN EXCESSIVE AMP DRAW WHEN ADEQUATE VENTILATION IGNORED

308. *ADEQUATE VENTILATION FOR H.V.A.C* RESIDENTIAL SPLIT SYSTEMS IS SIMPLE

IN ANY HOME U.S.A COLD AIR LEAVES THE SUPPLY REGISTERS(VENTS), COOLS THE SPACE, **THEN IS PULLED BACK THROUGH LARGE RETURN GRILL THAT CONTAINS THE AIR FILTER. THIS CRUCIAL PROCESS OF CIRCULATION IS KNOWN AS {EXCHANGING THE AIR} / {VENTILATION}**

309. *Through* **The Simple Art of Reducing Energy Consumption -The Definitive Guide-** *YOU HAVE NOW LEARNED:*
   a. *H.V.A.C STANDS FOR HEATING VENTILATION & AIR CONDITIONING*
   b. *H.V.A.C. SYSTEMS NATIONWIDE ARE TYPICALLY CLASSIFIED AS CENTRAL SPLIT SYSTEMS THAT HAVE ONE (1) INDOOR MACHINE PROVIDING HEATING, AND ONE (1) OUTDOOR MACHINE PROVIDING COOLING.*
   c. *IN ADDITION TO HEATING, YOUR INDOOR MACHINE ALSO PROVIDES {VENTILATION} OR {AIR EXCHANGE} THAT IS REQUIRED TO EXCHANGE THE AIR IN ANY SPACE SIX (6x) TIMES PER HOUR FOR PROPER PERFORMANCE & EFFICIENCY*
   d. *EVERY OUTDOOR MACHINE NATIONWIDE USES A ELECTRICAL COMPONENT CALLED A COMPRESSOR THAT CONSUMES BOTH LEGS OF VOLTAGE (240v) AND PRODUCES A AMP DRAW TO CIRCULATE REFRIGERANT IN A CONSTANT LOOP BETWEEN BOTH MACHINES OF A SPLIT SYSTEM DURING COOLING*
   e. *ADEQUATE VENTILATION IS THE KEY TO ENSURE EVERY RESIDENTIAL H.V.A.C. SPLIT SYSTEM IS PERFORMING WORK WITH PERFORMANCE AND EFFICIENCY YEARLY*

f. *HOMEOWNERS AND RENTERS ROB THEIR OWN H.V.A.C SYSTEMS OF PERFORMANCE AND EFFICIENCY WHEN INDOOR CRUCIAL ADEQUATE VENTILATION IS IGNORED.*

310. *WITH ALL THAT SAID PLEASE ALLOW ME TO* RECANT WHAT I OPENED STEP FOUR (4) WITH....

311. *YOU ARE USING THE WRONG AIR FILTER,* you are using the wrong air filter, *YOU ARE USING THE WRONG AIR FILTER,* you are using the wrong air filter, *YOU ARE USING THE WRONG AIR FILTER,* you are using the wrong air filter, *YOU ARE USING THE WRONG AIR FILTER,* you are using the wrong air filter, *YOU ARE USING THE WRONG AIR FILTER,* you are using the wrong air filter, *YOU ARE USING THE WRONG AIR FILTER,* you are using the wrong air filter, *YOU ARE USING THE WRONG AIR FILTER,* YOU ARE USING THE WRONG AIR FILTER

312. *OUR RESIDENTIAL AC SYSTEMS ARE DESIGNED TO USE FIBERGLASS* "CHEAP CHEAP GREEN" FILTERS THAT ARE NON-RESTRICTIVE.

313. *THE CHEAP, CHEAP, CHEAP, CHEAP, CHEAP GREEN FILTER YOU SEE AT WALMART AND BIG LOTS DO NOT RESTRICT THE AIRFLOW* THROUGH THE INDOOR MACHINE THAT CIRCULATES AND EXCHANGES THE AIR IN YOUR HOME

314. *WHEN YOU GO TO MAJOR HOME REPAIR STORES ALL YOU SEE* IS A WALL OF WHITE PLEATED FILTERS AS FAR AS THE EYE CAN SEE.

315. *THESE WHITE PLEATED FILTERS LOOK LIKE AN ACCORDIAN WHEN YOU LOOK AT THE FILTER MATERIAL* AND THE PACKAGING OF THE FILTER MAKES AN

ERRONEOUS PREPOSTEROUS ALLEGATION OF A NINETY (90) DAYS LIFE SPAN. TSK.

316. *WHITE PLEATED FILTERS REDUCE AIRFLOW INTO YOUR H.V.A.C SYSTEM BY FIFTY (50%) PERCENT WHEN THEY ARE BRAND NEW ON DAY ONE (1) OF ALLEGED NINETY (90) DAY LIFE SPAN*

317. *WHITE PLEATED FILTERS REDUCE THE CRUCIAL EXCHANGE OF INDOOR AIR BY YOUR INDOOR MACHINE BY SIXTY (65%) PERCENT ON DAY THIRTY (30) OF SO-CALLED DAY NINETY (90) DAY LIFE SPAN*

318. *WHITE PLEATED FILTERS REDUCE THE ADEQUATE VENTILATION OF YOUR SPLIT SYSTEM BY EIGHTY (80%) PERCENT ON DAY SIXTY (60) OF SUSPICIOUS NINETY (90) DAY LIFE SPAN*

319. *WHITE PLEATED FILTERS REDUCE AIRFLOW, AIR EXCHANGE AND VENTILATION NINETY (90%) PERCENT ON DAY NINETY (90) OF MAGICAL (90) DAY LIFESPAN*

320. *OUR RESIDENTIAL H.V.A.C. SPLIT SYSTEMS DEPEND ON AIRFLOW/VENTILATION/AIR EXCHANGE TO QUICKLY AND EFFICIENTLY COOL OUR HOMES.*

321. *HOMEOWNERS AND RENTERS THAT USE WHITE PLEATED FILTERS FORCE THEIR SPLIT SYSTEM TO OPERATE THIRTY (30) PERCENT LONGER AS THE INDOOR MACHINE STRUGGLES TO BREATHE.*

322. *UNDERSTAND THAT RESIDENTIAL H.V.A.C. INDOOR MACHINES MUST EXCHANGE THE AIR IN OUR HOMES AT LEAST SIX (6x) TIMES PER HOUR FOR PROPER HEATING AND COOLING.*

323. _GREEN NON-RESTRICTIVE FIBERGLASS FILTERS WERE ENGINEERED, DESIGNED AND FABRICATED TO_ MATCH THE PERFORMANCE SPECIFICATION OF RESIDENTIAL H.V.A.C. SYSTEMS

324. _HOMEOWNERS/RENTERS THAT USE GREEN FIBERGLASS FILTERS_ GAIN PROPER PERFORMANCE AND YEAR ROUND EFFICIENCY AS GREEN NON-RESTRICTIVE _FIBERGLASS AIR FILTERS WILL ALWAYS:_

    a. _ALLOW YOUR H.V.A.C SYSTEM TO BREATH_ THE HUGE VOLUME OF AIR THAT IS WAS ENGINEERED, DESIGNED ,AND FABRICATED TO BREATHE

    b. _AllOW YOUR INDOOR MACHINE TO EXCHANGE_ THE AIR IN YOUR HOME SIX (6x) TIMES PER HOUR

    c. _ALLOW YOUR SPLIT SYSTEM TO OPERATE THIRTY (30%) PERCENT LESS_ TO COOL YOUR HOME QUICKLY/ EFFICIENTLY

    d. _FORCE YOUR METER TO SPIN THIRTY (30%) PERCENT LESS_ TO COOL YOUR HOME WITH PROPER PERFORMANCE.

325. _DON'T BELIEVE ME? TRY THIS_ MAKE YOUR HOME AS QUIET AS POSSIBLE MAKE SURE UNIT IS ON.

326. _OPEN YOUR FILTER REGISTER AND JUST LOOK_ AT YOUR DIRTY DARK PLEATED FILTER

327. _OPEN YOUR EYES AND NOTICE_ HOW THE FILTER IS CONCAVE AND ALMOST BENDING INTO THE GRILL

328. _LISTEN CAREFULLY WITH YOUR EARS AS YOU CAN HEAR_ A FAINT HIGH PITCH WHINE OF RETURN AIR SQUEEZING PAST THE EDGES OF THE FILTER INTO THE INDOOR MACHINE

329. _NOW FOCUS ON THE SOUND OF THE FAINT HIGH PITCH WHINE_ OF AIR AS YOU PULL THE FILTER OUT OF THE RETURN GRILL....

330. _NOTICE THE MOMENT YOU OVERCAME THE RESISTANCE OF THE INDOOR MACHINE ATTEMPTING TO PULL THE FILTER INTO THE RETURN DUCT ITSELF,_ AND PULLED THE FILTER OUT A FEW AMAZING THINGS HAPPENED

331. _FIRST, THE FAINT WHINING NOISE OF AIR SQUEEZING PAST THE EDGES OF THE FILTER FRAME_ HAS COMPLETELY DISAPPEARED.

332. _SECOND, ALL YOU CAN HEAR IS THE DEEP LOUD SOUND OF EIGHTY (80%) MORE_ AIR NOW ENTERING THE RETURN GRILL UNOBSTRUCTED.

333. _FINALLY, USE YOUR SENSE OF TOUCH... AS YOU STAND THERE YOU CAN FEEL COLD AIR RUSHING PAST YOU FROM EVERY DIRECTION_ AS PROPER ADEQUATE VENTILATION IS NOW TAKING PLACE.... IT FEELS EXTREMELY NICE STANDING THERE.

334. _THIS IS BECAUSE THE SOCK IN THE FORM OF A PLEATED FILTER_ HAS BEEN REMOVED FROM THE MOUTH (RETURN FILTER GRILL) OF YOUR H.V.A.C. SYSTEM....

335. _THE VOLUME OF AIR THAT CAN NOW ENTER THE INDOOR MACHINE IS THE AMOUNT OF AIR_ THE INSIDE MACHINE WAS DESIGNED, CREATED AND ENGINEERED TO HAVE AT ALL TIMES, EVERY MINUTE OF THE DAY

336. _BY USING CHEAP FIBERGLASS FILTERS AND ALWAYS REPLACING MONTHLY, YOU CAN NOW PROPERLY_ RECIRCULATE/EXCHANGE THE AIR IN YOUR HOME SIX (6x) TIMES PER HOUR... FASCINATING STUFF I SAY.

337. _LAST (2) FUN FACT DEPICTING HOW PLEATED FILTERS ARE BOTH_ **POISONOUS AND DANGEROUS TO H.V.A.C. SYSTEMS AND THE HOMES THEY ARE HEATING & COOLING…**

338. _FIBERGLASS USED TO HAVE A DIFFERENT NAME WHEN THEY WERE INVENTED…_ **THEY USED TO BE CALLED "… FURNACE FILTERS…"**

339. _THIS IS BECAUSE COMBUSTION FURNACES BURN A FUEL SOURCE_ **AND CREATE INTENSE HEAT INSIDE A HEAT EXCHANGER….**

340. _ADEQUATE VENTILATION THEN MOVES THE AIR FROM INSIDE_ **THE HOME PAST THE HEAT EXCHANGER**

341. _THE HOMES CIRCULATING AIR ABSORBS THE HEAT_ **FROM THE HEAT EXCHANGER TO HEAT THE HOME.**

342. _WHEN THERE IS NOT ENOUGH AIR MOVING PAST THE HEAT EXCHANGER TO ABSORB THE INTENSE HEAT…_ **THE HEAT EXCHANGER WILL EVENTUALLY CRACK… ALLOWING DANGEROUS FUMES TO ENTER THE HOME…**

343. _ALL RESIDENTIAL H.V.A.C. SYSTEMS UTILIZED BLOWER MOTORS INSIDE_ **THE INDOOR MACHINE TO CIRCULATE THE AIR INSIDE YOUR HOME….**

344. _THESE BLOWER MOTORS ARE DAMAGED OVER TIME WHEN THEY ARE FORCED_ **TO OVERCOME THE RESISTANCE OF BREATHING WITH A PLEATED FILTER (SOCK) IN ITS MOUTH EVERY MINUTE DAILY**

345. _WHEN IN DOUBT, FOLLOW THE MONEY, MONEY, MONEY, PLEATED FILTERS ARE EXTREMELY COSTLY AND RIDICULOUSLY EXPENSIVE,_ **THEY DO OFFER A THREE (3) PACK OF FILTERS AT A BARGAIN PRICE… THE PLEATED**

MATERIAL IN THESE BARGAIN THREE (3) PACKS IS CHEAP AND RESTRICTS EVEN MORE AIR THAN THE PLEATED FILTERS THAT ARE SOLD IN SINGLE PACKS.

346. *CHEAP FIBERGLASS FILTERS ARE EXTREMELY CHEAP AND CAN BE PURCHASED ONLINE IN A PACK OF TWELVE ($12) FOR ABOUT TWENTY ($20) DOLLARS… IMAGINE THAT*

347. *Through **The Simple Art of Reducing Energy Consumption -The Definitive Guide-** YOU NOW UNDERSTAND PLEATED FILTERS WILL ALWAYS:*

    a. *DESTROY THE ABILITY FOR YOU H.V.A.C. TO EXCHANGE THE AIR IN YOUR HOME*

    b. *DESTROY PROPER CRUCIAL PERFORMANCE & EFFICIENCY OF EVERY H.V.A.C SYSTEM*

    c. *DESTROY PRICY IMPORTANT H.V.A.C. COMPONENTS SUCH AS HEAT EXCHANGERS AND INDOOR MACHINE MOTORS*

    d. *FORCE THE METER TO SPIN FASTER THIRTY (30%) MORE WHEN COOLING AND HEATING YOUR HOME ALL YEAR LONG.*

    e. *MAKE A FOOL OF RENTERS AND HOMEOWNERS WHO PAY EXORBITANT PRICES FOR FILTERS THAT ALLEGE A NINETY (90) LIFE SPAN AND DELIVER MECHANICAL FAILURES AND EXCESSIVE AMPDRAW ALL YEAR LONG INSTEAD OF A MAGICAL, WHIMSICAL, LUDACRIS NINETY (90) DAY LIFE SPAN.*

348. *AIR CONDITIONING IS VERY FORGIVING*

349. *H.V.A.C. SYSTEMS WILL WORK WHEN LOW ON REFRIGERANT*

350. *H.V.A.C. SYSTEMS WILL WORK WITH COMPRESSOR CAPACITORS HALF-SPENT AND OPERATING* **BELOW RATING THRESHOLDS**

351. *H.V.A.C. SYSTEMS WILL EVEN WORK WITH A SOCK STUFFED INTO* **ITS MOUTH**

352. *YES, THE H.V.A.C. SYSTEM WILL COOL THE HOME,* **BUT WHAT YOU LOOSE IS PERFORMANCE AND EFFICIENCY**

353. *TO EXPAND YOUR H.V.A.C. SYSTEM IS VERY FORGIVING, H.V.A.C. SYSTEMS CAN HEAT AND COOL YOUR HOME* **FOR YEARS WITHOUT REGULAR BI-ANNUAL MAINTENANCE**

354. *HOWEVER, LACK OF BASIC BI-ANNUAL MAINTENANCE WILL OVERTIME FORCE YOUR H.V.A.C.* **SYSTEM TO SHED ITS PERFORMANCE AND EFFICIENCY**

355. *THIS IS UNTIL A MECHANICAL OR ELECTRICAL FAILURE FINALLY PUTS YOUR HOME IN A "NO COOL" STATUS,* **NOW YOU ARE FORCED TO SPEND MONEY ON A SERVICE CALL TO REPAIR YOUR H.V.A.C. SYSTEM.**

356. *DISPATCHED TECH WILL MORE THAN LIKELY FIND A WASTED CAPACITOR THAT SHOULD HAVE BEEN REPLACED* **A YEAR AGO ON A BI-ANNUAL MAINTENANCE.**

357. *TECH WILL MORE THAN LIKELY FIND REFRIGERANT AT THE LOWEST OPERATING THRESHOLD* **(410A/108PSIG) AS REFRIGERANT GAUGES HAVE NOT BEEN ATTACHED TO MACHINE IN YEARS**

358. *TECH WILL MORE THAN LIKELY FIND BOTH OUTDOOR AND INDOOR COIL COVERED IN SAND, DIRT*, **GRIME, PET, AS BOTH COILS HAVE NOT BEEN MECHANICALLY OR CHEMICALLY CLEANED OR INSPECTED IN YEARS, AS A**

BI-ANNUAL MAINTENANCE HAS NEVER BEEN EXECUTED IN YEARS AND YEARS.

359. BOTH THE COILS ARE COVERED IN METAL FINS. WHEN THE FINS ARE DIRTY, GRIMEY, AND COVERED WITH PET HAIR AND GROWTH, THE AIR THAT PASSED THROUGH THE FINS HAS A HARDER TIME RELEASING AND ABSORBING HEAT FROM THE CIRCULATING REFRIGERANT THAT RUNS THROUGH THE COILS.

360. WHEN COILS AND FINS ARE CLEAN, AIR THAT PASSES THRU THEM WILL ABSORB AND RELEASE HEAT MUCH EASIER AS HOT AIR IS MAKING CONTACT WITH CLEAN SURFACE SPACE OF ALL THE FINS.

361. THIS WAY THE MAXIMUM HUMIDITY IS REMOVED FROM THE INDOOR AIR WITH ONLY ONE (1) COMPLETE CYCLE OF THE REFRIGERANT (PERFORMANCE AND EFFICIENCY)

362. H.V.A.C. IS VERY FORGIVING IT WILL WORK WITH ELECTRICAL CAPACITORS THAT ARE OPERATING WITH LOWER RATED VALUES THAN DESIGNED FOR YEARS AND YEARS.

363. CAPACITORS THAT ARE HALF SPENT WILL FORCE THE OUTDOOR MACHINE COMPRESSOR TO PRODUCE A HIGHER AMP DRAW... AND WE ALL KNOW HOW I FEEL ABOUT EXCESSIVE UNNECESSARY HIGH AMP DRAWS.

364. H.V.A.C IS VERY FORGIVING, IT WILL WORK WITH A SOCK IN ITS MOUTH (BRAND NEW PLEATED FILTER)

365. THIS ALL MEANS, YES THE H.V.A.C. SYSTEM WILL COOL THE HOME BUT, IT HAS TO STAY ON DANG NEAR 24/7 TO DO A MEDIOCRE JOB OF COOLING AND HEATING THE

HOME, THAT ALL EQUATES TO MORE AND MORE AMP DRAW BEING PRODUCED ALL DANG YEAR LONG.

366. *THE H.V.A.C. SYSTEM STRUGGLES ALL DAY, ALL NIGHT, ALL WEEK, ALL YEAR AS IT PRODUCES:*

    a. *A HIGHER AMP DRAW ALL YEAR LONG*

    b. *AN EXCESSIVE AVOIDABLE AMP DRAW ALL YEAR LONG*

367. *WHAT IS AN IMMEDIATE QUICK FIX? USE ONLY THIN GREEN FIBERGLASS FILTERS THAT YOUR MACHINES WERE ENGINEERED TO OPERATE WITH*

368. *REPLACE FIBERGLASS FILTERS MONTHLY*

369. *BOTTOM LINE IS THE THINNER YOUR FILTER, THE FASTER YOUR THERMOSTAT REACHES SET POINT.*

370. *IF ALL YOU HAVE EVER USED IS WHITE PLEATED FILTERS IN YOUR H.V.A.C. SYSTEM, THEN YOU HAVE NEVER EVEN MET YOUR H.V.A.C. SYSTEM. YOU HAVE NEVER EXPERIENCED YOUR H.V.A.C. SYSTEM OPERATING AT PEAK PERFORMANCE AND EFFICIENCY…. EVER.*

371. *Through **The Simple Art of Reducing Energy Consumption -The Definitive Guide- YOU HAVE NOW LEARNED:***

    a. *H.V.A.C. SYSTEMS WILL SHED PERFORMANCE AND EFFICIENCY WHEN BI-ANNUAL MAINTENANCE IS IGNORED FOR YEARS AND YEARS.*

    b. *CAPACITORS OPERATING UNDER VALUE WILL FORCE COMPRESSOR TO PULL HIGHER AMP DRAW*

    c. *DIRTY COILS ON SPLIT SYSTEMS WILL FORCE LONGER AMP DRAWS YEARLY*

    d. _A SOCK(PLEATED FILTER) STUFFED INTO YOUR H.V.A.C. SYSTEM'S MOUTH_ WILL FORCE LONGER AMP DRAWS ALL YEAR LONG.

    e. _NEGLECTED BI-ANNUAL MAINTENANCE AND LACK OF ADEQUATE VENTILATION WILL FORCE EXCESSIVE AMP DRAW YEAR ROUND AND FORCE_ H.V.A.C. SYSTEM TO SHED ITS PERFORMANCE AND EFFICIENCY ALL YEAR LONG AND SIMPLY RUN ALL DAY TO BARELY COOL THE HOME.

372. _SO……. WHICH BEDROOM IS THE HOTTEST_ ROOM IN YOUR HOME? HMMMMMMMMMM?

373. _FINALLY WE MUST CORRECT AIR IMBALANCES BY TURNING THE HOTTEST ROOMS IN_ THE HOME INTO THE COLDEST ROOMS IN THE HOME

374. _THIS IS ACHIEVED BY ADDING ACTIVE RETURN AIR VENTS_ TO EVERY BEDROOM.

375. _RETURNS THAT ARE INSTALLED INTO EACH BEDROOM MUST BE ACTIVE RETURNS,_ NOT PASSIVE RETURNS.

376. _ACTIVE RETURNS HAVE A DEDICATED DUCT THAT TRAVELS ALL THE WAY BACK TO THE RETURN_ AIR PLENUM ATTACHED TO THE INDOOR MACHINE.

377. _PASSIVE RETURNS ARE A SIMPLE HOLE_ AND GRILLS CUT ABOVE THE DOOR.

378. _TYPICALLY THE ROOMS THAT SUFFER_ ARE THE FARTHEST ROOMS FROM THE AIR HANDLER.

379. _ACTIVE RETURNS MUST HAVE THEIR OWN DEDICATED DUCT THAT TRAVELS FAR FAR AWAY_ TO THE RETURN AIR PLENUM ATTACHED TO THE INDOOR MACHINE.

380. *PASSIVE RETURNS OVER THE DOOR VIA TWO (2) FLAT GRILLS WILL PROVIDE* **LITTLE TO NO COOLING GAINS TO THE HOT ROOMS.**

381. *SEMI-PASSIVE RETURNS ARE DUCTED TO A NEARBY RETURN AIR DISTRIBUTION BOX THAT HOLDS THE MAIN FILTER* **WILL YIELD MARGINAL COOLING GAINS TO HOT BEDROOMS.**

382. *FULLY ACTIVE RETURNS THAT USE LONG DEDICATED DUCTS* **TO TRAVEL TO THE RETURN SIDE PLENUM OF THE AIR HANDLER WILL YIELD ENORMOUS COOLING GAINS TO THE HOTTEST ROOMS.**

383. *FOR ANY ROOM TO HAVE A CHANCE TO COOL PROPERLY, THE AIR IN THAT ROOM MUST BE* **EXCHANGED OR REPLACED AT LEAST SIX (6x) TIMES PER HOUR.**

384. *WHEN BEDROOMS DO NOT HAVE ACTIVE RETURN AIR VENT, THE BEDROOM WILL ALWAYS BE HOT* **ONCE THE BEDROOM DOOR IS CLOSED AS THE AIR BECOMES STALE IN THE ROOM.**

385. *THIS IS WHY TEENAGERS' ROOMS TYPICALLY SMELL LIKE GYM SOCKS AS THEY ALWAYS KEEP THE DOOR CLOSED,* **THIS BEDROOM IS NOT EXCHANGING THE AIR IN THE ROOM AT LEAST SIX(6) TIMES PER HOUR.**

386. *THIS HOT ROOM NEEDS TO HAVE AN ACTIVE RETURN AIR DUCT* **INSTALLED NEAR THE ENTRY OF DOOR OF THE ROOM.**

387. *AS FAR AS ATTIC INSULATION, I RECOMMEND TOP TIER* **SPRAY FOAM INSULATION COMPANY.**

388. *Through* **The Simple Art of Reducing Energy Consumption -The Definitive Guide-** *YOU NOW COMPREHEND TO REDUCE THE*

ENERGY CONSUMPTION NEEDED TO HEAT AND COOL YOUR HOME, YOU ABSOLUTELY MUST ALWAYS:

    a. STAY AWAY FROM PLEATED FILTERS AT ALL COST

    b. USE AND REPLACE GREEN FIBERGLASS FILTERS EVERY THIRTY (30) DAYS TO ENSURE ADEQUATE VENTILATION

    c. HAVE BI-ANNUAL MAINTENANCES PERFORMED ON SCHEDULE YEARLY

    d. LEAVE ALL BEDROOM DOORS OPEN

    e. HAVE ACTIVE RETURNS INSTALLED IN EVERY BEDROOM.

    f. WHEN APPLICABLE, ALWAYS SELECT A HEAT PUMP NEW OUTDOOR MACHINE INSTALL

389. *WE ARE WINDING DOWN STEP FOUR (4) WITH THE TOP SIX (6) NATIONAL BRANDS AND HOW LONG-TERM AMP DRAW IS IMPACTED*

390. *FIRST ALLOW ME TO WHAT DEFINES A NATIONAL BRAND. THE FOLLOWING SIX (6) BRANDS HAVE DEDICATED MACHINE WAREHOUSES AND FULLY STAFFED PARTS COUNTERS IN EVERY MAJOR U.S. CITY.*

391. *EVERY OTHER BRANDS BELOW THE NATIONAL BRAND SELL THEIR MACHINES AND PARTS AT 3RD PARTY DEALERS THAT HAVE LIMITED WAREHOUSES AND PARTS COUNTERS. THIS EQUATES OUT TO MORE NATIONAL BACKORDERS FOR REPAIR PARTS AND INFERIOR MACHINES BRANDS THAT WERE DESIGNED AND ENGINEERED TO BE INEXPENSIVE, NOT SUPERIOR.*

392. 393. *NOW I GIVE YOU THE SIX (6) SUPERIOR NATIONAL BRANDS AND WHAT MAKES EACH ONE SPECIAL. THESE*

NATIONAL BRANDS ARE PRESENTED IN ORDER OF HOW LONG THE BRAND HAS BEEN ON THE MARKET…. NOT PERSONAL PREFERENCE.

393. *A FEW MAJOR BRANDS HAVE MACHINES THAT ARE BUILT IN THEIR FACTORIES; HOWEVER, THESE MACHINES ARE STAMPED WITH A DIFFERENT NAME BADGE, THIS IS DONE TO OFFER AFFORDABLE OPTIONS TO CONTRACTORS WHO CHOOSE TO INSTALL MAJOR BRANDS, BUT NEED A LOWER TIER OPTION OF A PARTICULAR BRAND AS THE CUSTOMER HAS LIMITED FUNDS,*

394. *I NOW PRESENT THE TOP NATIONAL BRANDS AND THE LOWER TIER BADGES THAT ARE BUILT IN THEIR FACTORIES, ALONG WITH SPECIAL FACTS THAT ARE UNIQUE TO EACH BRAND.*

395. *REMEMBER, THE FOLLOWING BRANDS ARE PRESENTED IN ORDER OF HOW LONG THE BRAND HAS BEEN ON THE MARKET…. NOT PERSONAL PREFERENCE.*

396. *NUMBER ONE (1) CARRIER/BRYANT/PAYNE ALL MANUFACTURED AT CARRIER FACTORIES. WILLIS CARRIER IS THE MAN CREDITED WITH INVENTING RESIDENTIAL H.V.A.C. SYSTEMS. BIG AND WELL STAFFED WAREHOUSES AND PARTS COUNTERS NATIONWIDE.*

397. *NUMBER TWO (2) TRANE/AMERICAN STANDARD (NOT AMERISTAR) TRANE HANDS DOWN LEAD THE INDUSTRY WITH THE MOST ON-GOING RESEARCH AND DEVELOPMENT AT ALL TIMES, SUPERIOR MATERIAL FROM THE INTERNALS OF THE COMPRESSOR TO THE PROPRIETARY POLY VINYL INDOOR MACHINE CABINETS THAT REQUIRE NO TRADITIONAL INSULATION*

PADDING (MEANING IF INDOOR MACHINE HAS A CLOGGED DRAIN LINE, THE INSULATION INSIDE THE INDOOR MACHINE WILL NOT BECOME SOAKED WITH WATER,,,, AS THERE IS NO INSULATION NEEDED TO PAD THE INSIDE OF THE INDOOR MACHINE CABINET). NATIONWIDE PARTS HOUSES ARE BEAUTIFUL BUILDINGS BUILT TO PROVIDE COMFORT TO H.V.A.C. CONTRACTORS (FREE SODA MACHINES, POPCORN, REGULAR CONTRACTOR APPRECIATION COOKOUTS AND FREE LUNCHES) ALL MACHINES ARE BUILT TO BE EASILY SERVICED AND MAINTAINED FOR THE LIFE OF THE MACHINE.

398. *NUMBER THREE (3) LENNOX, ANOTHER ONE OF THE ORIGINAL BRANDS THAT HAS BEEN MANUFACTURING MACHINES SINCE THE INCEPTION OF RESIDENTIAL H.V.A.C. SYSTEMS. THIS BRAND IS FREQUENTLY FOUND IN RESIDENTIAL NEW CONSTRUCTION NATIONWIDE*

399. *NUMBER FOUR (4) YORK, A LONG TIME MANUFACTURE OF RESIDENTIAL H.V.A.C. SYSTEMS THAT HAS ONE UNIQUE FEATURE NO OTHER BRAND OFFERS, YORK MACHINES ARE THE ONLY MAJOR BRAND THAT IS EXCLUSIVELY BUILT IN HERSHEY PENNSYLVANIA, OTHER BRANDS MY HAVE LARGE FACTORIES IN THE AMERICA; HOWEVER, THE MAJORITY OF THE MACHINE IS BUILT OVERSEAS, THEN FINALLY "ASSEMBLED" IN THE AMERICA. EVERY YORK MACHINE IS BUILT IN AMERICA BY AMERICANS.*

400. *NUMBER FIVE (5) RHEEM, THIS BRAND CAN BOAST THAT THEY MAKE THE PHYSICALLY SMALLEST INDOOR MACHINE CABINETS…. THIS IS CRUCIAL IN TEENY TINY*

ATTICS AND TEENY TINY CLOSETS WHERE A SMALL INDOOR MACHINE IS NEEDED

401. *NUMBER SIX (6) GOODMAN/GMC. THE MOST AFFORDABLE OF THE NATIONAL BRANDS AND HAVE RECENTLY PAIRED WITH DIAKEN (PROLIFIC COMMERCIAL H.V.A.C. BRAND) TO BRING A STRONG TWELVE (12) YEAR LONG PART AND LABOR WARRANTIES THAT CERTAIN H.V.A.C. CONTRACTORS* **CAN OFFER THEIR CUSTOMERS. NOT EVERY H.V.A.C. CONTRACTOR WILL OFFER THE TWELVE (12) YEARS PART AND LABOR WARRANTIES AS THEY ARE EXTREMELY EXPENSIVE… BUT ABSOLUTELY WORTH IT.**

    a. *IT IS THIS STATE OF FLORIDA H.V.A.C. CONTRACTORS OPINION THAT TRANE MACHINES KEEP A LOWER AMP DRAW OVER THE LIFE OF THE MACHINES… HENCE "NOTHING STOPS A TRANE"*

402. *Finally I close with a referral SO FAR YOU WILL NEED:*

    a. *A PLUMBING CONTRACTOR to turn down your electric hot water tank.*

    b. *AN ELECTRICAL CONTRACTOR to install a dial timer on the electric hot water tank.*

    c. *AN H.V.A.C. CONTRACTOR to clean your coils, replace half dead capacitors, clear your drain line every 6 months and balance your refrigerant*

    d. *A DRYER VENT COMPANY to clear the exhaust vent*

403. *In this case I nominate a Goliath H.V.A.C, Plumbing, Electrical company that offers* **all three services…**

404. *No stand alone AC company can compete* **with a Goliath AC company.**

405. *Large Goliath companies have the deep pockets to employ na-tionwide vetted employees, they sell the most superior brands* **with superior 10 year full labor warranties (industry standard is only 1 year full labor warranty).**

406. *Goliath companies offer service plans that include AC, electrical and plumbing maintenance* **into one attractive bi annual main-tenance contract .**

407. *Goliath companies care for their employees and customers be-cause they can afford it* **and refuse to operate at a mediocre level.**

408. *Make no mistake, Goliath company prices are higher than the rest because* **they truly operate at an elite level.**

409. *Don't call a Goliath ac company for a* **good price...**

410. *Call them for absolute accountability, prestige, and complete* **peace of mind.**

411. *One last thing. the Energy we consume today is reflected on the next power bill cycle...* **so be patient & consistent with the techniques I have shared with you.**

412. *The next bill may not fully reflect your energy savings, However the bill after next* **will show you all your glorious savings**

413. *Through The Simple Art of Reducing Energy Consumption -The Definitive Guide-* **You have taken back FULL CONTROL of your power bill w/ Extreme Prejudice and Absolute Accuracy** *AS YOU ARE NOW:*
    a. *COOKING and baking while consuming 80% less energy*
    b. *heating the water in your home consuming 50% less energy*
    c. *drying the clothes in your home consuming 50% less energy*
    d. *cooling and heating your home consuming 30% less energy.*

414. *My work here* **is all done….**

415. *The poltergeist* **has been cast out….**

416. *This house…. Is clear.*

417. *I am extremely happy as you now understand the electrical principles of amp draw* **and energy consumption.**

418. *I am beyond thrilled as you will NEVER NEVER NEVER* **unknowingly CONSUME excessive ENERGY**

419. *This Definitive Guide Was created to help you* **protect and provide for your family**

420. *I do not have a checking account let alone a savings account.* **I know what it's like to put items back on the shelf at the grocery store.**

421. *I know what it's like to wake up to a* **repossessed car.**

422. *I know what it's like to steal a handful of strawberries* **from Publix to feed my son.**

423. *I Created this definitive guide as I know what suffering means…* **so many other families are suffering**

424. *This definitive guide was created and formatted in email form for mass communication* **not for profit, no link no download, no physical book YET, all to help all those who are watching their children slowly be starved by high power bills**

425. *EMERGENCY PROCEDURES TO REDUCE ENERGY CONSUMPTION BY NINETY (90%) PERCENT* **EFFECTIVE IMMEDIATELY**

426. *These procedures are for the Americans* **on the brink of losing everything...**

427. *These are procedures for my precious American senior citizens* **who are going on 6 months of eating dog food to survive...**

428. *These are procedures for my families* **who were struggling before 2020...**

429. *These are procedures for my impoverished families* **with 4 kids who have not brought a gallon of milk home in a year…**

430. *These are procedures for my young single mothers who are forced to do things to strangers to keep those routine astronomical power bills paid on time* **or lose the babies when those people come knocking on the door because the power has been off for weeks.**

431. *I told you all why I started this guide,* **to prove others wrong….**

432. 433. *all of you suffering pain and anguish are the reason i FINISHED this guide…* **all of you are the reason I have spent the last 10 days straight formatting this guide into a free email I have not showered, slept, or relaxed in 10 days as i knew your needs were greater than mine…all of you are reason i have been a man possessed as i format this guide for you….the faster its finished,, the faster it gets sent to every major news and media outlets all of you are the reason my face is leaking, pouring, streaming as I type these final paragraphs.**

433. *I'm sorry for your pain, listen to me closely now* **and let's end this nightmare together…**

434. ****RULES OF ENGAGEMENT****

435. *YOU WILL NEVER REPLACE A BREAKER IN YOUR BREAKER PANEL*

436. *YOU WILL NEVER ALLOW ANYONE TO "UPSIZE" A BREAKER PANEL BECAUSE IT KEEPS SNAPPING SNAPPING SNAPPING*

437. *HOMEOWNERS, YOU WILL NEVER ALLOW ANY HUMAN BEING EXCEPT A STATE LICENCED ELECTRICAL CONTRACTOR TOUCH YOUR BREAKER BOX AT ALL*

438. *Stand up and open your breaker box. Renters may find the breaker box in the hallway. Open the panel, don't be scared…* **there is nothing to be afraid of… I am right here next to you…**

439. *I know the idea of touching the breaker box terrifies you… I promise you have nothing to fear… The powerful helix of my DNA is now & forever intertwined into yours…* **You are more powerful in this moment than you will ever know… Trust me now… Let's do this together.**

440. *Look at the breakers, notice there are thick breakers, and thin breakers. Thick breakers are for the electrical appliances that consume both legs of voltage to produce heat and high amp draw,* **typically Oven, Hot water, Dryer AC and Heat Now one by one, Turn all the thick breakers into the off position**

441. *Next, look at the (thin) breakers, that provide power to the bed-rooms. Go open your fridge so the light is on, now go and turn on the bathroom light, return to breaker box. Now, one by one,* **Turn off each thin breaker as you turn off the thin breakers, keep an eye on the fridge light and bathroom light as you flip the thin breakers off.**

442. *The only 2 breakers that should be on now, are the fridge/kitchen and bathroom breaker, now go buy the countertop oven* **as the kitchen typically has 1 breaker for the fridge and the kitchen countertop receptacles (outlets)**

443. *Now you can cook for your family producing extremely little amp draw Now you can cook for your family* **while reducing energy consumption to the absolute maximum.**

444. *Purchase a small window ac unit from Walmart for 150. Pay a qualified handyman to install it in your bedroom. remove all the furniture from this room. Put all the bed mattresses in this*

room, keep the door to the room closed so the window unit can turn the room into an ice cube. **At night turn the thin breaker on that powers your bedroom. Now you can sleep comfortably with your family while producing extremely little amp draw. Now you can sleep comfortably with your family while reducing energy consumption to the maximum**

445. *If you just begged 3 different people in tears to please loan you money for a small window unit… You will need about five (5) more dollars for the install materials,* **pick up one Phillips starhead (NOT flathead) Phillips cheap screwdriver and a cheap roll of original duct tape.**

446. *A small window unit install is a heavy* **heavy heavy job.**

447. *Someone must help with putting the window unit* **in the cart, then trunk, then bedroom…**

448. *My Seniors WILL NOT do this by themselves* **or even with the two of you together.**

449. *My seniors will put on their Sunday finest, and head to walmart…* **Once onsite, grab the cart and into the service counter line you go….**

450. *When you get to the counter, ask the young human* **that you please need three (3) things:**

    a. *two store associates to escort you to the aisle where the window ac units are.*

    b. *For the two store associates to load the window unit into the cart and push the cart itself to the service desk where window unit shall be paid for*

    c. *And finally for the two associates to push the cart to your car and load the window ac unit into your trunk or backseat*

451. *If the associate that shows up happens to be another one of my seniors named Jim, please tell Jim i said, that window unit is the heaviest box with those small dimension in that entire store and is extremely difficult to pull back out of the cart to put up on the counter to be scanned,* **so be sure to put the window ac unit into the cart so the barcode is up…. And make sure the 2ⁿᵈ associate is prepared for a proper team lift.**

452. *Once my seniors arrive back home with the precious cargo, go inside and grab a sheet,* **return to the vehicle and cover the window A.C. with sheet, lock the car doors and back inside you go.**

453. *Upon dropping the car keys into the bowl and setting the receipt on the counter…. Relax a minute,* **have a cold drink and grab the rolodex**

454. *We are seeking a qualified handy-man. Once you get one on the horn, explain you need an estimate to arrive, bring the window unit in from the car and install the window ac unit in the new ice cube,,,* **I mean the bedroom… don't be very surprised if the labor quote is more than the price of the window A.C. unit… once you confirm the appointment tell them not to forget the dolly cart so they can get the window A.C. safely to your bedroom.**

455. *My seniors are extremely important to who I am and who I was raised to be… my fathers name is Carlos Rubio, he was fifty-five (55) the day I was born… growing up he taught me his two life hacks… number one (1) always respect the law, and number two (2) always have common courtesy for everyone around you…* **I remember being seven (7) years old and giggling because he would say his two life hacks back to back and his voice would drop a quarter octave lower with each word till he sounded like a dad robot at the end…** *I remember being fifteen(15) and my stoic*

father who never cried in front of me was holding back tears as he was reporting to me that for the first time in history Seniors in Florida were having to eat dog food to cover medicines... i remember seeing him in physical pain as he raised his voice with emotion... **i remember when he finished his sentence he looked away to hide his emotion of pain and despair as he knew other seniors were in pain he could do nothing about it...** *My father is the one who forced me to attend Tampa Bay Tech High School when i was fifteen (15) he is the reason this definitive guide exist on any level... When i was thirty-one (31) My family and I put my father in the earth... It was that moment of my life in 2011 I knew i had to find the path my father always told me i would find,* **by 2012 i passed the trade portion of the Florida AC contractor state exam.... 2013 I would pass my business and finance state exam completing all state required exams. In feb 2017 i would finally earn the state AC contractors license my father told me would one day earn.... I had to put my father into the earth to come to life myself...** *Thank you resting father... I am now forty-two (42) and will make damn sure none of my precious seniors on fixed incomes ever in their life stream tears of misery as they open a can of dog food for the thirteenth (13) day in a row to keep the escalating astronomical power bills.... never.*

456. *To my fellow americans in the most pain* **and misery hear me now:**

457. *my mentor published* <u>Alternative Medicine the Definitive Guide</u> *over twenty years ago,, in that guide i read something powerful..*

458. *I read about the sensation* **of "hopelessness"**

459. *Hopelessness is the most destructive sensation in the world. It will eat you alive from the inside out.* **It will release chemicals in your brain that will slowly destroy your mind, body and Soul...**

With the suffering you have all endured these past years, all you know is hopelessness…. All you feel is hopelessness. You wake up and go to sleep defeated as the chains of hopelessness silently suffocate the will to live out of you… THAT ENDS NOW…

460. *As you stand in your dark home looking at the breaker box that only has two breakers on;* **You don't have to "hope" things get better. THEY WILL get better…**

461. *As time passes you don't have to "hope" you have money left over for groceries* **to feed your kids. YOU WILL have enough money for groceries…**

462. *You don't have to hope to regain control of your power bills…* **with only two breakers on, you NOW HAVE complete control.**

463. *As you stand there in your dark home looking at the open panel,* **I want you to feel "Powerful"**

464. *YOU HAVE THE POWER..* **YOU DECIDE WHEN THAT METER SPINS**

465. *As you stand there in your dark home looking at the open panel,* **i want you feel "DOMINATION"**

466. *YOU DOMINATE THE AMPDRAW YOUR HOME PRODUCES, YOU CHOOSE, DICTATE AND DOMINATE WHEN THAT METER SPINS…* **THAT METER WILL NEVER SPIN AGAIN UNLESS YOU SAY IT DOES…. YOU NOW STAND OVER THAT BREAKER BOX WITH ABSOLUTE AUTHORITY. With only two breakers on, YOU NOW CRUSH THE LARYNX OF THE SAME SPINNING METER THAT HAS BEEN TRYING TO STRANGLE YOU FOR 3 YEARS NOW**

467. *NOW,,pick up your chin, dry your eyes and go hug your babies..* **explain things will be different moving forward BUT things will get better….**

468. *OUR babies will believe you as they have been watching you slip away* **into hopelessness for so long now...**

469. *YOUR babies will see, hear, feel, and absorb* **your newfound emotions of power, pride and domination..**

470. *TEACH your babies what you learned in this definitive guide.* **Teach your babies how to protect themselves from excessive high amp draw...**

471. *FINAL THOUGHTS AMERICA... we can never control the amount of money the power company charges us for power...* **What we can control is the amount of energy we consume. Nobody can ever**

take that from us... Ever... Now go tell everyone in your Universe what just happened here:

472. <u>*Through*</u> <u>*The Simple Art of Reducing Energy Consumption -The Definitive Guide-*</u> **Your Nightmare is Over......**

Thank you all **for being patient and open-minded with my first publication. I have so many people to thank...first and foremost:**

Thank you Dr. Wendy Coughlin at DrWendyCoughlin.com **for teaching me how to draft in a linear fashion Dr. C....you gave me the blueprint and most important template i have ever followed...I could feel you next to me as i typed every single line....you are myHeroine... I have told you this several times i will say it once more.....- To Valhalla- ;}**

Thank you Retired Honorable Irene Sullivan Esq. **for restoring order to my world & saving my universe.**

Thank you David Anton Esq. and Kay at AntonLegalGroup.com **for your guidance and protection...Hey Kay...(less words) :}**

Thank you W.F. Casey Ebsary II Esq. at CentralLaw.com **for keeping a extended wing of protection over me for 10 years now**

Thank you Dr. Troy Noonan, Dr. Will Homan, and Dr. JL Durchin at MHMgroup.com **for creating the best version of me**

Thank you Dr. Deepak Chopra **for setting a high bar and leaving footprints in the sand for me to follow...we both have definitive guides now:D**

Thank you Randy, Cindy & Rene Leblanc **for teaching me everything I have just shared.**

Thank you Fernando, Donna, Marc, & David Falquez **for teaching me drive, ambition & sophistication through higher education.**

Thank you Dr. Jordan Peterson **for teaching me how to grow teeth.**

Thank you Amazon Kindle **for creating a free platform for people like me.**

Thank you Google and gmail **for the ability to format this guide in bright colors for free**

Thank you Paul & Donna Poffenbaugh, Sara Aryinfar-Eikman & Dr. Robert Smeed **for your lifetime of friendship.**

Thank you Brian & Leslie Thompson at SideSplittersComedy.com **for keeping me close to your hearts while teaching me to never be ashamed for anything my heart wants.**

*Thank you Wes Watson at WesWatson.com **for teaching me to never be ashamed of my***

emotions as emotions are Energy in Motion.

*Thank you JB Ball at Ball4president.com **for showing me how to manifest dreams into reality.***

*Thank you Randy Nelson at NelsonStoneWorks.com **for the motivation***

*Thank you John allen at Mrballenfoundation.org **for teaching me the power of social media.***

*Thank you Jonathon Wilson at Baybrickpavers.com **for your patience.***

*Thank you to Bubba the Love Sponge at show@bubbaarmy.com **BUBBA!!!, It was Your Bubba Army that picked me up and shared me with the world. Thank you with all my heart.** @ Bubba Army- **We Do This Together.***

Thank you to all the brilliant minds and beautiful souls at Archway Publishing from Simon & Schuster

*To my beautiful brilliant son Christian, Thank you for choosing me as your dad...**You did this son..Every Character building day we had over the past 3.5 years is what built the character needed to make this a possibility. Not one drop of pain was in Vain. everything happened exactly as it had to... You just helped millions & millions of people, my beautiful boy...I knew you could do it:) Always shoot for the moon in a neighboring constellation my son.. Always remember...Winning is in your blood-You were born with what it takes. I will always be next to you my son, in this life and beyond... #MITclassOf2031***

Thank you to my sister Patricia, my Mother beautiful Marisol, And my resting father Carlos Rubio,

Thank you America

-Your friendly local
State of Florida licensed AC contractor
John Rubio, Pro se Litigant
Xoxoxoxoxooxoxox I love you all.
facebook.com/johncarlos1981

"…. It is Almost As if Routine High Power Bills Are Devouring Americans Alive…Something Must Be Done… Now…"

August 1st, 2023 MARKS THIRTY-NINE(39) CONSECUTIVE MONTHS OF: **high power bills emancipating annihilation upon a convalescing American nation… Our all but gone elderly population is suffering on a day-to-day basis. Our younger generation are working hard to hardly eat on weekends. Not even school aged children are spared the grim painful realities of routine astronomical power bills.**

August 1st, 2023 MARKS SEVEN(7) SEQUENTIAL MONTHS: **A young couple in the Big Apple is disparaged w/ hunger pangs and novel anxiety… They have responsibly always paid their power bill in full. Today is seven straight months of Not Stocking their pantry with sufficient groceries & spirits. The silent affliction of subtle starvation examines the resilience of the aging high school sweethearts. Primal screams begin to fill their uptown NEW YORK apartment. They fight as to whose idea it was to start touching the savings two years ago…**

…{DON'T FORGET}. THEY ARE GOING ON SEVEN(7)BACK-TO-BACK MONTHS OF: **drinking tap water while barking**

and bickering over bargain basement food that never seems to last.

August 1st, 2023 MARKS FOUR(4) CHRONOLOGICAL MONTHS OF: **No Power for millions of displaced MIDWESTERN families… Three consecutive years of escalating power bills has effectively rendered Midwestern families subhuman swine. Overt vulgar dehumanization of men, women & children has eclipsed integration as Midwestern families are now routinely reduced to huddling as livestock for survival. The freezing MIDWEST climate & eager midnight** moon conspire with calculated collusion and control by coercion. Precise execution of a perfectly pristine sunset plunge the broken MIDWEST mother into the dark ages. Intense cold, perverse peril and the torment of Siberian torture irrevocably induce suicidal thoughts in accordance with psychosis. All she can hear in the freezing dark is her infant daughter's lingering chest infection getting worse instead of better...

{DON'T FORGET} FOUR(4) MONTHS AGO: Her Power was Interrupted Weeks Before Winter Over Unpaid Astronomical Power Bills Accrued Over Summer...

August 1st, 2023 MARKS EIGHTEEN(18) MONTHS UNTIL: Millions upon millions of FLORIDA seniors wake up to depleted & drained savings accounts... These are OUR precious elderly citizens who built the foundations of modern civilization for future generations. These are OUR brave Americans who created our nation with unwavering fortitude and strength. Now they Cannot Stop Chest Pains that intensify as they stare demoralized at another five hundred and sixty-two ($562) monthly high power bill...

...{DON'T FORGET} ONLY EIGHTEEN(18) MONTHS LEFT UNTIL: Depletion Of Their Final FLORIDA Savings Account....

August 1st, 2023 MARKS THREE WEEKS UNTIL: Parents in CALIFORNIA witness their children commence the upcoming 2023 school year with tattered jeans and jackets from 2021... These parents have honorably worked hard to keep escalating summer power bills paid in full-on time for decades. Prosperous CALIFORNIANS are *known to simply work more if it means never touching the savings account. These particularly persistent parents work sixty-five (65) hours weekly keeping major ends met and miniature mouths fed. They work hard and are grateful to consider themselves the "Lucky Ones"*

…{DON'T FORGET}… ONLY THREE(3) MONTHS UNTIL: These Parents face the Inevitable Indecent Proposal of paying harsh early withdrawal penalties commencing the defilement of their life savings OR bringing home less and less groceries in perpetuity.

HOW CAN HOMEOWNERS AND RENTERS EMERGE EFFECTIVELY to CT HIGH POWER BILLS IN HALF TODAY?

HOW CAN A CONFUSED NATION CHAOTICALLY CONSUMED IN CONSUMPTION IMMEDIATELY CUT POWER BILLS IN HALF TODAY?

COUNTLESS WITNESS ACCOUNTS ILLUSTRATING A NAIVE NATION IN PAIN HAS GIVEN RISE TO THE PUBLICATION OF THIS DEFINITIVE GUIDE.

ENDLESS TESTIMONIALS THAT DEPICT THE SUFFRAGE OF AMERICANS HAS GIVEN RISE TO THE PUBLICATION OF THIS DEFINITIVE GUIDE.

EMPOWERING MY NATION WITH SIMPLE METHODS TO ERADICATE MONTHLY HIGH POWER BILLS WITH EXTREME PREJUDICE HAS GIVEN RISE TO THE PUBLICATION OF THIS DEFINIIVE GUIDE.

TEACHING EVERY AMERICAN HOW TO DOMINATE THEIR

HIGH POWER BILLS WITH CONFIDENCE, POWER AND PRIDE HAS GIVEN RISE TO THE PUBLICATION:

THE SIMPLE ART OF REDUCING ENERGY CONSUMPTION -THE DEFINITIVE GUIDE-

MR. RUBIO has a DEGREE in H.V.A.C, ADVANCED DIPLOMAS in AIR CONDITIONING/REFRIGERATION, GRADUATED NINETY-SEVENTH (97th) PERCENTILE of his AIR CONDITIONING PROGRAM earning his H.V.A.C TRADE SPECIALIZED DIPLOMA FromTAMPA BAY TECH HIGH SCHOOL c/o 1999

He is a STATE OF FLORIDA LICENSED AIR CONDITIONING CONTRACTOR, 2002 E P A UNIVERSAL LICENSE RECIPIENT and is REGULATED by the FLORIDA DEPT of BUSINESS and PROFESSIONAL REGULATION in the application of his H.V.A.C HEATING, VENTILATION, AIR- CONDITIONING-COMPANY throughout the STATE OF FLORIDA

MR. RUBIO is an ADJUNCT PROFESSOR of RESIDENTIAL AIR CONDITIONING at various FLORIDA INSTITUTIONS of EDUCATION AND LECTURES FREQUENTLY on topics including, but not limited to:

> *a. INDOOR AIR QUALITY in residential applications*
> *b. QUANTUM THERMODYNAMICS*
> *c. REFRIGERATION CYCLE THEORY*
> *d. REDUCTION of ENERGY CONSUMPTION W/SUPERHEAT AND SUBCOOL PRINCIPLES*

MR. RUBIO invested ten(10) FORMATIVE YEARS an APARTMENT SUPERVISOR during which he EDUCATED TENANTS how to TAKE

BACK CONTROL from REPEATED ROUTINE MONTHLY HIGH POWER BILLS

HE DISPLAYS PROCLIVITIES and AFFINITY for HOLISTIC MEDICINE has Credits In GENERAL STUDIES, MEDICAL TERMINOLOGY, HUMAN ANATOMY and PHYSIOLOGY, and is a DEVOUT 20-YEAR PROTEGE FOLLOWING THE TEACHINGS OF DR. JOAN BORYSENKO' S <u>MINDING the BODY MENDING the MIND</u> as well as DR. DEEPAK CHOPRA'S highly coveted: <u>ALTERNATIVE MEDICINE -THE DEFINITIVE GUIDE-</u>

MR. RUBIO has been conducting residential AIR CONDITIONING SERVICES AND SHARING REDUCTION OF ENERGY CONSUMPTION PRACTICES with his PRECIOUS FLORIDA HOMEOWNERS AND RENTERS for Thirty(30) Years.

He has led a DEDICATED DRIVEN LIFE of AMBITIOUS SCHOLARLY ENDEAVORS THROUGH COMMITMENT FOCUS and SHEER WILL.

CHARACTER BUILDING HARDSHIPS DEVASTATING TRIBULATIONS have been turned into VISION BOARDS AND JET FUEL then promptly met with ABSOLUTE ASCENSION

His SKILL SET, REPUTATION, and PASSION to positively impact humanity IRREVOCABLY and UNEQUIVOCALLY Endorse and Authenticate MR. RUBIO The CLEAR and CONVINCING PINNACLE AUTHORITY on RESIDENTIAL AIR CONDITIONING

.... Please Make No Mistake....YOU WILL NOT ENCOUNTER A MORE QUALIFIED air conditioning contractor in the entire NORTHERN HEMISPHERE

HIS DNA HELIX EFFECTIVELY DEFINES THE VERY ESSENCE OF AVANT GARDE...

Mr. Rubio's Aforementioned Credentials not only Bears a Significant Relationship to but is Inextricably Intertwined w/ the publication of **THE SIMPLE ART OF REDUCING ENERGY CONSUMPTION -THE DEFINITIVE GUIDE-**

Author Biography

 **John Rubio**, C.A.C. state of Florida licensed air conditioning contractor.

Mr Rubio's debut publication masterfully authenticates a comprehensive Definitive Guide cleverly calculated to easily ingrain simple permanent procedures cutting American residential power bills in half effective immediately.

He honorably stands before you as a state of Florida A/C contractor with a degree in residential air conditioning, advanced diplomas in H.V.A.C and as an adjunct senior professor of residential air conditioning at various Florida institutions of higher education.

Mr. Rubio has been conducting air conditioning services and sharing energy reduction consumption practices with his Florida renters/homeowners for thirty years.

His character building hardships and devastating tribulations are perpetually reverse engineered into astounding vision boards and synthesized rocket fuel...then met with absolute ascension....you will Not encounter a more qualified air conditioning contractor in the entire northern hemisphere.... The generational wisdom coded in the helix of his DNA induce manifestations of avant-garde...

Printed in the United States
by Baker & Taylor Publisher Services